MODERN QUILT MAGIC

5 Parlor Tricks to Expand Your Piecing Skills

★ 17 Captivating Projects ★

Victoria Findlay Wolfe

stashBOOKS®
an imprint of C&T Publishing

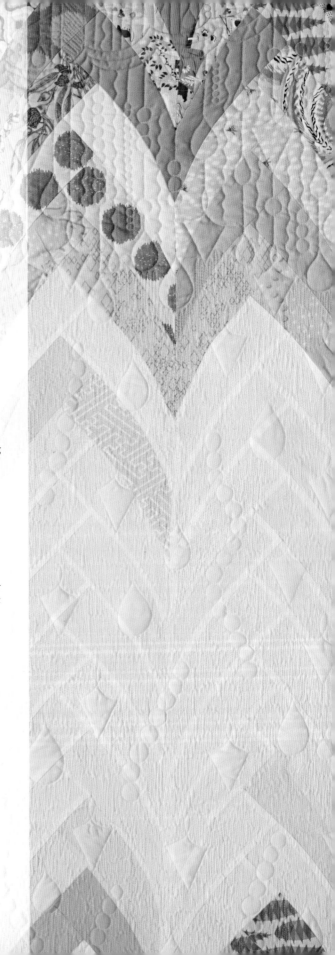

Text and artwork copyright © 2017 by Victoria Findlay Wolfe

Photography and artwork copyright © 2017 by C&T Publishing, Inc.

Publisher: Amy Marson

Creative Director: Gailen Runge

Editor: Liz Aneloski

Technical Editors: Debbie Rodgers and Helen Frost

Cover/Book Designer: April Mostek

Production Coordinator: Zinnia Heinzmann

Production Editor: Jennifer Warren

Illustrator: Aliza Shalit

Photo Assistants: Carly Jean Marin and Mai Yong Vang

Hand Model: Kristi Visser

Style photography by Lucy Glover and instructional photography by Diane Pedersen
of C&T Publishing, Inc., unless otherwise noted

Published by Stash Books, an imprint of C&T Publishing, Inc., P.O. Box 1456,
Lafayette, CA 94549

Library of Congress Cataloging-in-Publication Data

Names: Wolfe, Victoria Findlay, 1970- author.

Title: Modern quilt magic : 5 parlor tricks to expand your piecing skills -
17 captivating projects / Victoria Findlay Wolfe.

Description: Lafayette, CA : C&T Publishing, Inc., [2017]

Identifiers: LCCN 2016059348 | ISBN 9781617455087 (soft cover)

Subjects: LCSH: Patchwork--Patterns. | Quilting--Patterns.

Classification: LCC TT835 .W6426 2017 | DDC 746.46--dc23

LC record available at https://lccn.loc.gov/2016059348

Printed in the USA

10 9 8 7 6 5 4 3 2

Dedication

To Kim Hryniewicz, Laura Clark, and Shelly Pagliai.

Without you three, my head would be lost in the "quilted" clouds. . . .

Acknowledgments

I must thank the following individuals and companies:

My darling husband, Michael—you are so patient with me and my ideas. My daughter—you have become a great help to me with videos and even in hand sewing. (Though you say you are not a quilter, that seed has been planted. Sorry about that!) I love you both so much.

Shelly Pagliai—thank you again! Your work, your humor, and your friendship are a perfect fit.

Linda Welters of the University of Rhode Island and the Rhode Island Quilt Documentation Project, for the beautiful herringbone quilt image.

Aurifil, for all my luscious thread!

Juki, for my fabulous machines.

My SSQ pals (you know who you are)—always fabulous and supportive.

The C&T Publishing staff, for your support!

CONTENTS

PARLOR TRICK ONE:
Partial-Seam Construction   13

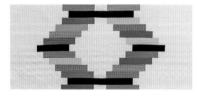

PARLOR TRICK TWO:
Blocks with Partial Seams   61

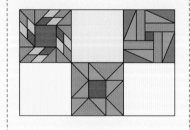

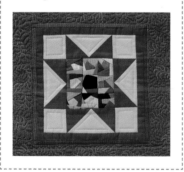

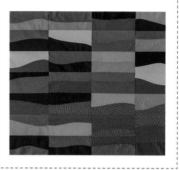
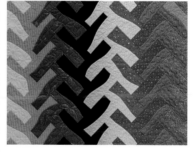

INTRODUCTION

Parlor Tricks

A *parlor trick*, historically, described a simple magic trick performed as a way to awaken and encourage curiosity in an audience. The trick pulled the crowd in, bent their mind, and made them ask, *"How* was that done?"

Why parlor tricks in this book? When I'm teaching, I try to find the one thing that will take the fear out of learning. Most of the "tricks" I show are quilting tricks that people missed in their quilting education—or have simply forgotten. Surprisingly, many of these tricks take no more than fifteen minutes to learn! That's what I want to share with you in this book.

Making what some call "difficult" quilts is really not hard to do at all. Taking just a few minutes to learn a new quilting or sewing trick can take your quilting skills to a whole new level.

Want to make a quilt that can knock the socks off of the friends and family you share your work with? Does seeing something that looks impressive and difficult (but isn't) inspire you? Do you want to know how? Here are the answers!

With a tiny bit of know-how, you will see that these quilts are easier than you think. The ability to make a powerful quilt statement lies in your hands. We don't have to share all our secrets to those outside the quilt-obsessed community; just say, "Thank you!" when they applaud you for your work!

This book also serves as a reference of standard quilting techniques that help make your quilting process easier. Having taught so much these last few years, I have come to realize which quilting tricks many people have not learned or are afraid of, even though they may have been sewing for 30 years. Nothing in this book is actually difficult to do. With some simple instruction and a release of fear and negative thinking, you can take on new challenges and have some fun!

When I first started quilting (feverishly? obsessively? joyfully?), I wanted to learn everything I could. Having come from a sewing family, I did not know I should be afraid of any technique. I'd already sewn curves and partial "set-in" seams when I was making clothes. It's standard practice! So making more complex quilts didn't seem like a big stretch for me. Making quilts that look complicated—without actually being difficult—is very satisfying and a great part of what I love about quilting.

Everything but the Kitchen Sink, by Victoria Findlay Wolfe, quilted by Linda Sekerak, 2009, 89˝ × 93˝

Herringbone Strip Quilt, by Nancy Carpenter Hixson (1844–1927), late 1890s, 88½″ × 83½″

Cotton top and back, hand-pieced, tied. Private collection. Rhode Island Quilt Documentation Project #96.
Illustrated in the book *Down by the Old Mill Stream: Quilts in Rhode Island*.

When I first saw an antique herringbone quilt, someone asked, "How on earth was this quilt made?" I quickly jumped in—because one, I didn't know any better as far as my quilting practices went, and two, I had just made *Everything but the Kitchen Sink* (page 7), which is assembled completely with partial seams and incorporates curves, Y-seams, and miniature piecing (everything that I want to cover in this book). So figuring out how to piece the quilt in question didn't seem like a big mystery to me.

I want to focus mostly on partial seams, but I'm giving you the information you need to master curves and Y-seams, to boot! Once you have conquered those techniques, you'll be able to join all your leftover blocks into your own "Everything but the Kitchen Sink" style of quilt. I give you permission to make it up as you go along!

So here we are … you're going to be pushed visually. You will learn new skill sets, take a few baby steps, and then be able to play out all the options! Soon you'll see how you can make a "*Wow!* How did you do *that*?" quilt.

Why would you want to learn something that looks difficult? Because what looks hard at first glance is often not as challenging as you think when you take a closer look. Looking is a big factor in learning a new trick. Instead of discounting it as something really difficult and thinking, "Why waste my time with it?" take a few minutes to learn something new. You'll build your confidence and patience: two things we all need a little bit more of, right? Self-doubt lies heavily in each of us, but we can change that by embracing and conquering a new challenge. Learning a new task can quickly retrain your eyes to see things differently and widen your horizons creatively. Plus, better construction of your quilts makes your confidence soar!

Get clear about your artistic integrity. Visually you can make a fabulous looking quilt, but how is your piecing? Before you think I'm going all "quilt police" on you, let me say this: You are your own quilt police. You care if the point matches or doesn't; you care or know that a seam did not line up! No one else will care. (And if they do, tell them, "Lighten up, Sunshine; it's just fabric.") You get to decide how much of that is important to you, but my job is to show you how to get awesome results.

If you're taking the time to learn a new trick, the more quilts you make, the more your skill set grows. When I'm teaching, I have learned it's often very basic sewing elements that people are missing. When I hear, "I can't keep my points on stars…." and the like, I know that one quick little tip can take your skill set leaps forward!

★ TIP *Want to know a secret? Patterns and templates are usually designed with a ¼˝ seam. If you don't want to cut off your star points, you do need to sew a precise ¼˝ seam. After the seam is sewn, you should have ¼˝ of fabric beyond your point. Pinning is also key. (I hear all those groans!) Pinning your seams to line up and pressing your seam allowances in opposite directions so they nestle together (all of those things we learned and often ignore) make for a better-constructed quilt. There will be more on that later, in the Y-seam parlor trick (page 84).*

I want to focus on two things with the quilts and instructions in this book: techniques (or "tricks," as I like to call them) and *looking*. It's not just sleight of hand; a well-played parlor trick and a fair amount of looking will take you far, not just in these quilts but also in every other quilt you make.

How to Look

I find that we are trained to look at what is in front of us but get stuck because our brain tells us something different. We have our preconceived ideas about what we like and what we don't. Often, people can rattle off a long list of what they don't like but a shorter list of what they *do*.

I often hear people say in class, "Oh, I don't like orange," or, "I don't like brown." But that might be just what their quilt needs! If you take the time to retrain your eye to look at the colors in front of you and how they react to the entire collection of fabrics you've chosen—as well as looking inside each individual color in a print—you may find that orange or brown are there and will work great in your quilt! Often that orange might just have the brightness you need to perk up your quilt, or that brown may have the right amount of depth needed to add movement to your project.

Keep Your Options Open

Remember to look with your eyes and not with your head. Put your layout up on a wall to look at it and take photos of it. Step back to look at your work. I guarantee it doesn't look the same as it does in your brain!

It's like trying on clothes: In your head, you think that something might not look great on you. Then you try it on, look at it, and realize it looks amazing! Avoid saying, "I don't think it will look good." Cut the fabric, lay it out, and look at it. Then make your decision.

Don't fall into the trap of what you *don't* like. It is a venomous black hole that will hold you back creatively. Focus on what do you like. Even if you think it's the ugliest fabric you've ever seen, can you look inside the print and find one color you like individually, by itself? There you go. You just changed your thinking by taking one baby step.

Think positively. Look closely. Quilting is fun!

TIP *Look for my glasses symbol throughout the book for more ways to push yourself further in looking.*

To break down looking even further, think about a pattern in black and white lines, much like the grown-up coloring books that are so popular these days. You are in control over how you are going to fill each individual space with color. Instead of one color, maybe there will be five! In the case of a quilt pattern, maybe it is improvising another shape within the pattern piece, or making a different block that can then be cut down and added to a space.

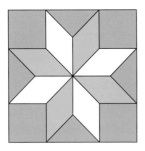 

When I'm working on a pattern, I look at each individual shape and decide how I am going to fill that space with color. How can I add a new story to the quilt that might not have been originally planned?

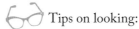 Tips on looking:

- Identify what you like.

- Ask, "What if?"

- Take photos and look at the colors through the lens.

- Looking is often different than your mind's perception of it. Your *mind* can't see, but your *eyes* do.

- Try to find the one *treat fabric*—a fabric that is not quite a perfect fit but adds interest—while you look around the quilt. Identify a color that you wouldn't expect to put into the palette.

- Think of the basic shape you are working with. How you can change the information within that shape?

TIP *Before you attempt the quilts in this book, try the smaller class projects first. Once you master the technique, the rest becomes a breeze!*

PARLOR TRICK ONE
PARTIAL-SEAM CONSTRUCTION

Herringbone

Generally we see partial-seam blocks when a block is designed around a square for the spinning visual motion (see Parlor Trick Two: Blocks with Partial Seams, page 61). But not always! I want to start you off with this herringbone pattern because it is easier to learn in small steps. I focused my newest series of quilts on this pattern. I am fascinated by how difficult it looks—when in actuality it is really not hard at all.

Most of us are familiar with braid quilts, a similar pattern that is started by making the overlapping rows. As a last step, the edges of braided rows are cu off straight for ease when sewing the rows together.

Oh Baby! is a standard braid quilt. The edges of the braid are cut off, making a straight seam to join the rows.

But here, in this herringbone quilt, we are *leaving* the edges and using partial seams to incorporate them into the design of the quilt. Boom! There's your *wow* factor!

Oh Baby!, by Victoria Findlay Wolfe, 2016, 27½″ × 34″

Using partial seams to sew edges together makes for more complex-looking quilts.

CUTTING

From a variety of fabrics:

- Cut 24 light strips 2″ × 8″.
- Cut 24 dark strips 2″ × 8″.

CONSTRUCT THE ROWS

1. With right sides together and the ends aligned, sew the short end of a light strip to the side of a dark strip, forming an L. *Fig. A*

2. Flip open and press (or finger-press) the seam allowance up. *Fig. B*

★ **TIP** *Press only the portion you've sewn—do not press all the way to the sides of the row. The direction your seam allowances are pressed is very important for ease of construction and for your piece to lie flat at the end!*

A.

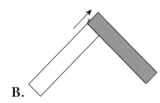

B.

3. With right sides together and the top ends aligned, sew a light strip to the left/top side of the unit. About 2″ from the end of the strip you are adding, stop sewing and do a short backstitch to secure. This is a partial seam. *Fig. C*

C.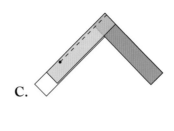

4. Flip open and press the seam allowance up. *Fig. D*

D.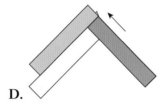

5. Sew a dark strip to the right/ top side of the unit. *Fig. E*

E.

6. Continue adding strips, alternating left-side lights and right-side darks, 12 on each side. These are all partial seams. Each seam should be open on the outside edges about 2″ from the end, and the seam allowances should be pressed up. *Fig. F*

F.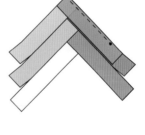

7. Now try another row reversed: left-side darks and right-side lights, 12 on each side. *Fig. G*

G.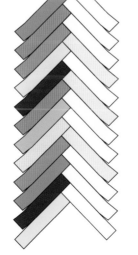

JOIN THE ROWS

Work from the *top* of the rows down, joining and completing the partial seams. *Fig. A*

1. Starting from the left side of the quilt, pick up the first 2 rows to begin the braided seams. *Fig. B*

2. Flip the second row *up* to align with the first short seam, right sides together. The 2 rows will form an L shape. Pull the rest of the strips out of the way and sew the end of the strip in the first row to the top side of the strip in the second row. *Fig. C*

3. Open and finger-press the seam allowance up (toward the top of the rows). Position the rows for the next seam. *Fig. D*

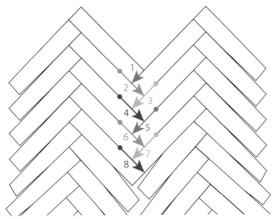

A. Braided seam order to join rows

4. Fold *down* the second row and the top strip in the first row. Finish this partial seam, keeping the remaining strips out of the way. *Fig. E*

5. Open and finger-press the seam allowance up (toward the top of the rows). Position the rows for the next seam. *Fig. F*

6. Fold the second row *up* along the seam under its top strip. Finish this partial seam, keeping the remaining strips out of the way. *Fig. G*

7. Open and finger-press the seam allowance up (toward the top of the rows). Position the rows for the next seam. *Fig. H*

8. Fold *down* the second row and the top 2 strips in the first row. Finish this partial seam, keeping the remaining strips out of the way. Finger-press the seam allowance up. Continue joining the rows in this manner. *Fig. I*

9. Once you have sewn all the rows together, *finish sewing the open seams on the outside rows.*

10. Lightly press the quilt top, being careful not to stretch the fabrics.

11. Trim the sides of the quilt top even with the lower inside point of each strip using a long ruler. (It will look like you are cutting off a long row of triangles.)

12. Trim the top and bottom edges even with the innermost points. *Fig. J*

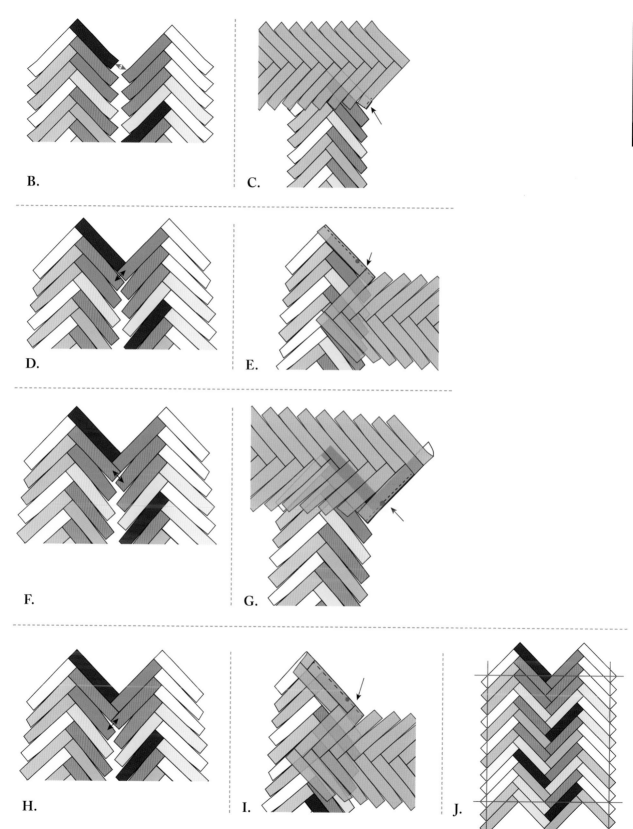

B.

C.

D.

E.

F.

G.

H.

I.

J.

CLASS PROJECT: HERRINGBONE PILLOW

By Victoria Findlay Wolfe, 2016, 20˝ × 20˝

Make a herringbone piece from Parlor Trick One: Partial-Seam Construction (page 13) and turn it into a pillow! Mastering this skill prepares you for the larger projects in this chapter.

MATERIALS

Herringbone piece from Parlor Trick One (page 13)

Muslin: ⅔ yard for pillow quilt backing

Batting: 22˝ × 22˝

Pillow backing: ⅔ yard

20˝ pillow form

Binding: ⅓ yard

CUTTING

Muslin: Cut a square 22˝ × 22˝.

Pillow backing: Cut 2 rectangles 20½˝ × 15˝.

Pillow Finishing

1. Layer the herringbone piece, batting, and muslin.

2. Quilt as desired.

3. Trim all of the layers even with the herringbone pieced top.

4. On one long edge of each pillow backing rectangle, press under ⅜˝; then press under 3˝. Topstitch on both long sides of the 3˝ section, close to the edge, creating a cleanly finished band. *Fig. A*

5. Lay the *wrong* sides together with the front quilted panel. The back panels with the finished edges will overlap in the middle.

6. Sew around all 4 sides, pivoting in the corners to turn. I like to reinforce the edges on the sides where the back pieces overlap. In the seam allowance, add another line of stitching in the overlap areas. *Fig. B*

7. Cut the binding and apply it to the front, just as for a quilt. Fold around to the back and hand stitch down.

8. Insert a 20˝ pillow form through the back overlap. It can be removed easily for cleaning.

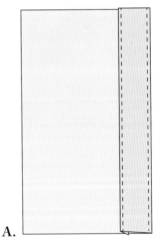

A.

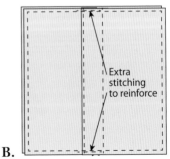

Extra stitching to reinforce

B.

LAVENDER WALLS

Finished quilt: 115½˝ × 100½˝ (before quilting)

By Victoria Findlay Wolfe, quilted by Shelly Pagliai, 2016

When I first saw the *Herringbone Strip Quilt* (page 8) and the woman asked everyone, "How was this made?" it bent my mind, and I was immediately sucked in! I set about making my first attempt at the quilt. I purchased 30 yards of fabric (all from 1 vendor at a quilt show!) to make it for my bed. I had just painted my apartment walls a very light lavender and wanted the perfect quilt. Well, perfect is relative … I am only perfect in my imperfections!

The same process used to make the herringbone piece from Parlor Trick One: Partial-Seam Construction (page 13) is used to make this quilt. Selecting a set of light and dark prints and alternating their value gives the quilt depth and movement. I love to drop in a treat color to pop here and there, which helps lead the eye around the quilt. My treat color in this quilt is green.

I call it *adding treats*: It's finding something that is not quite a perfect fit but adds interest while you look around the quilt … because who really makes perfect quilts? (Anyone? *Anyone?*) When selecting a treat fabric, it helps if you find one that has multiple colors already used in the chosen fabrics. I used a Kaffe Fassett fabric that had blues, greens, and purples. The blues and purples already in the quilt made sense with this fabric, and I could

play with my treat of green placed strategically throughout the quilt. Your treat color can be used very sparingly for effect.

I've used mostly reproduction fabrics in this quilt, along with fabrics that have been in my stash for ages. I also tossed in some modern fabrics, making this a great quilt for stash busting. Mix it up! Have fun playing with color. One thing you may find is what you consider a dark may also work in the light section, and vice versa. Allow crossover colors on purpose for added design interest!

TIP *I was anxious to get this quilt done, but making a king-size quilt gets tedious! For this size, I timed myself to see how long it took for me to make one row. Each day I set aside that amount of time to make one row.*

I make all my rows first, grabbing strips randomly. Random, you will find, is not as random as you think! You will instinctively start pulling in a particular pattern. (Trust me; I know!) So make all your rows first. Next you can play with the order in which the rows will go together. Look for patterns in color that land in the same place, and switch rows around until you have an equally distributed palette of color.

MATERIALS

This is a scrappy quilt, so amounts of fabrics vary. This quilt uses mostly quarter-yard cuts of many different fabrics.

Fabrics	Crib (42″ × 60″)	Twin (73½″ × 86″)	Full (84″ × 88″)	Queen (94½″ × 94″)	King (115½″ × 100½″)
Row layout	62 strips × 4 rows	86 strips × 7 rows	88 strips × 8 rows	94 strips × 9 rows	100 strips × 11 rows
Lights/whites/stripes	2 yards total	4 yards total	4½ yards total	5¼ yards total	6¾ yards total
Darks/mediums/reds	2 yards total	4 yards total	4¼ yards total	5¼ yards total	6¾ yards total
Backing	2¾ yards	5¼ yards	7⅝ yards	8½ yards	10½ yards
Batting	48″ × 66″	80″ × 92″	90″ × 94″	101″ × 100″	122″ × 107″
Binding	½ yard	¾ yard	⅞ yard	⅞ yard	1 yard

CUTTING

Fabric*	Crib	Twin	Full	Queen	King
Lights**	124	301	352	423	550
Darks**	124	301	352	423	550

*This is the exact number of strips needed for each size layout, but it is useful to cut extras so you can play with color.
**Strips are cut 2″ × 8″.

Construct the Rows

The approximate finished row width is 10½″. You will be working from the *bottom*, alternating the left (dark) and right (light) sides to build each row.

1. With right sides together and the ends aligned, sew the short end of a dark strip to the side of a light strip, forming an L. *Fig. A*

A.

2. Flip open and press (or finger-press) the seam allowance up.

Lightly press the portion you've sewn—don't press all the way to the sides of the row. The direction your seam allowances are pressed is very important for ease of construction and for your quilt to lie flat at the end! *Fig. B*

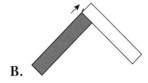

B.

NOTE > As you add each strip, sew across the end and side of the previous strips. Make sure to keep the raw edges together along the edge of the whole strip, especially at the intersection of the previous seam.

3. With right sides together and the top ends aligned, sew a dark strip to the left/top side of the unit. About 2″ from the end of the strip being added, stop sewing and do a short back-stitch to secure. This is a partial seam. *Fig. C*

4. Flip open and press the seam allowance up. *Fig. D*

5. In the same way as Steps 3 and 4, sew a light strip to the right/top side of the unit. *Fig. E*

6. Continue adding strips, alternating left-side darks and right-side lights, until the row reaches the number of strips needed for the desired layout. These are all partial seams. Each seam should be open on the outside edge about 2″ from the end, and the seam allowances should be pressed up. *Fig. F*

7. Sew the remaining rows needed for your desired layout. Start at the *bottom* of each row with a left (dark) strip each time. *Fig. G*

C. 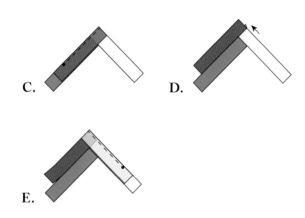 D.

E.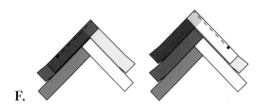

F.

G.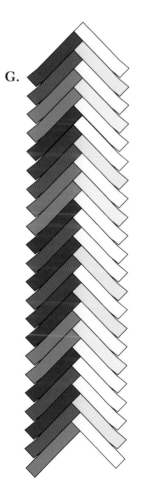

Join the Rows

Work from the *top* of the rows down, joining and completing the partial seams. *Fig. H*

1. Starting from the left side of the quilt, pick up the first 2 rows to begin the braided seams. (See the diagram for an overview of the braided seam order to join rows.) *Fig. I*

2. Flip the second row *up* to align with the first short seam, right sides together. The 2 rows will form an L shape. Pull the rest of the strips out of the way and sew the end of the strip in the first row to the top side of the strip in the second row. *Fig. J*

3. Open and finger-press the seam allowance up (toward the top of the rows). Position the rows for the next seam. *Fig. K*

4. Fold *down* the second row and the top strip in the first row. Finish this partial seam, keeping the remaining strips out of the way. *Fig. L*

 It can help to place a pin in the intersecting seam allowance to hold it in the correct direction as you sew the new seam.

5. Open and finger-press the seam allowance up (toward the top of the rows). Position the rows for the next seam. *Fig. M*

6. Fold the second row *up* along the seam under its top strip. Finish this partial seam, keeping the remaining strips out of the way. *Fig. N*

7. Open and finger-press the seam allowance up (toward the top of the rows). Position the rows for the next seam. *Fig. O*

8. Fold *down* the second row and the top 2 strips in the first row. Finish this partial seam, keeping the remaining strips out of the way. *Fig. P*

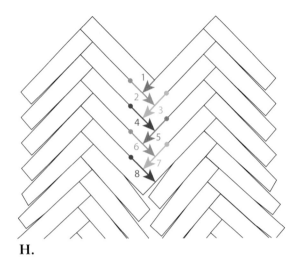

H.

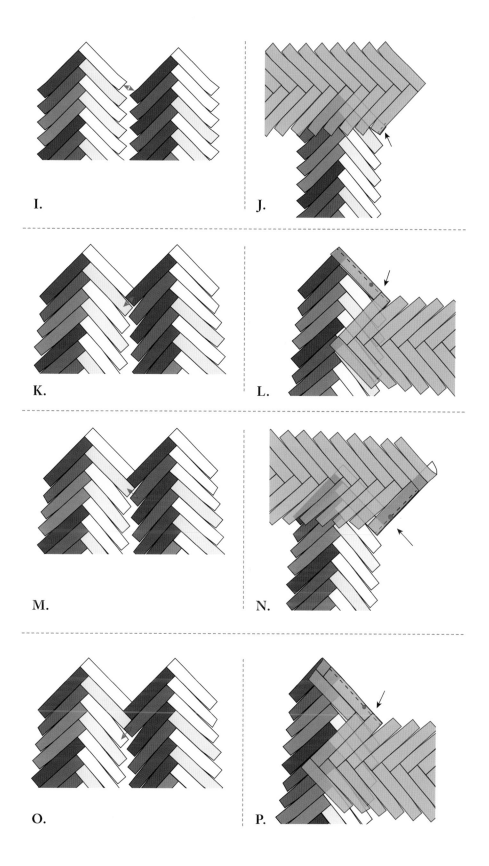

I.

J.

K.

L.

M.

N.

O.

P.

9. Open and finger-press the seam allowance up (toward the top of the rows).

10. Continue completing the partial seams, alternating the right- and left-leaning seams in the established order. Finger-press the seam allowances up after each seam. If needed, place a pin to hold the seam allowance in that direction.

11. When the 2 rows are sewn together, carefully press all the seam allowances up.

12. Repeat Steps 1–11 to join the remaining rows together in pairs. Sew the pairs of rows together, and then sew those sections together, until you've completed the quilt top.

NOTE > If you sew the rows in pairs first (rather than continuing to add one row to a growing unit each time), there is less fabric to flip up, flip down, and wrestle around with when you're sewing those alternating partial seams.

13. Once you have sewn all the rows together, *finish sewing the open seams on the outside rows.*

14. Lightly press the quilt top, being careful not to stretch the fabrics.

15. Lining up with a long ruler, trim the sides of the quilt top even with the lower inside point of each strip. (It will look like you are cutting off a long row of triangles.)

16. Trim the top and bottom edges even with the innermost points.

Row layout for king-size quilt

Finishing

1. Lightly press the quilt top, being careful not to stretch the fabrics.

2. Layer, quilt, and bind.

AT THE CROSSROADS OF
MODERN AND GRAND*

Finished quilt: 73½″ × 86″ (before quilting)

Also known as Lite Brite

By Victoria Findlay Wolfe, quilted by Shelly Pagliai, 2016

I love how the herringbone pattern can change completely by using a different color placement. We are looking at the same quilt pattern as before.

Notice how it changed visually when I dropped color into the light rectangles. I liked the idea of separating the color into paths and really focusing the whites into a negative space. It looks and feels so completely different from *Lavender Walls* (page 19) just because of the brights and solids that are popping into all the rows.

Popping the bright, saturated color into the white and light rows adds to the visual effect, helping guide your eye around the quilt. You want to look at the white rows, then at each pop of color individually. When you see the entire quilt, you see the movement. Next you focus on the darker areas, and your eye goes to the seventh row, the *darkest* green in the upper middle section, and then your eye may drop down to just below the middle, to a slightly lighter green.

Color placement is like telling a good story: You lead the person through the quilt by giving just enough information to deliver a happy ending. Give the quilt a squint, and see what else it is telling you. What else might your quilt need? The V's in the pattern could have been part of the design focus. I could have made a continuing path of color in one area across the quilt. I chose to play with the direction of the lines by switching to the color placement in the middle row. Visually, everything is pointing you to the center row of the quilt. A similar concept can be used to scale this quilt to whatever size you choose to make.

MATERIALS

Fabrics	Crib (42″ × 60″)	Twin (73½″ × 86″)	Full (84″ × 88″)	Queen (94½″ × 94″)	King (115½″ × 100½″)
Row layout	62 strips × 4 rows	86 strips × 7 rows	88 strips × 8 rows	94 strips × 9 rows	100 strips × 11 rows
Lights/ whites	2 yards total	4 yards total	4½ yards total	5¼ yards total	6¾ yards total
Bright prints and solids	2 yards total	4 yards total	4½ yards total	5¼ yards total	6¾ yards total
Backing	2¾ yards	5¼ yards	7⅝ yards	8½ yards	10½ yards
Batting	48″ × 66″	80″ × 92″	90″ × 94″	101″ × 100″	122″ × 107″
Binding	½ yard	¾ yard	⅞ yard	⅞ yard	1 yard

CUTTING

Fabric	Crib	Twin	Full	Queen	King
Lights*	112	317	328	442	556
Brights*	136	285	376	404	544

*Strips are cut 2″ × 8″.

NOTE > When changing the size of this pattern, you will want to reconfigure your color placement according to how many rows you are making. Refer to the herringbone diagram in Coloring Design Pages (page 116).

This is the approximate number of strips needed for each size layout, but it is useful to cut extras so you have some to play with.

Construction

This quilt is constructed just like *Lavender Walls* (page 19). However, the color placement is different and the strips are arranged in rows that point downward rather than up. So start at the *top* when constructing each row, and start at the *bottom* when joining the rows together.

To make this twin-size quilt, use the row layout diagram (at right) and refer to the directions for *Lavender Walls* (page 19).

Start constructing rows from top.

Row layout for twin-size quilt

Joining rows starts from bottom.

MARION LANE

Finished quilt: 89˝ × 97˝ (before quilting)

By Victoria Findlay Wolfe, quilted by Shelly Pagliai, 2016

With this quilt I had three goals: stash busting, using my Japanese fabrics, and pushing the scale. By scale, I mean using wide and narrow variations that will still braid together into the herringbone pattern. Using a black-and-white braid as a border in my earlier quilt, *Big Red: The Farmer takes a Wife*, inspired me to take that idea further.

Big Red: The Farmer Takes a Wife, by Victoria Findlay Wolfe, quilted by Shelly Pagliai, 2014, 82″ × 82″

What I love about this quilt is the play going on in two different directions. Horizontally, there are peaks or upside down V's, and in the herringbone braid pattern, the black and white works its way vertically up the quilt.

Now notice the color placement. The yellows are below the halfway mark of the quilt. Each row has a set that stands out slightly more than the others, which helps the horizontal play of pattern. Next, you are drawn to the two bright pink and green fabrics in the upper right-hand corner.

In my quilt designs, I like to point people where I want them to look. By doing so, I hope they will come closer and see all the crazy prints I included in this quilt! Novelty, text, reproduction, modern, stripes, you name it … this quilt has it. It is like walking down a street doing a little window-shopping, which is exactly why I named this quilt *Marion Lane* (a street I visited on one of my many travels). If you look closely enough, you may find the title stitched into the quilt as well!

MATERIALS

This is a scrappy quilt, so amounts of fabrics vary. This quilt uses mostly quarter-yard cuts of many different fabrics with larger amounts of black and white.

Fabrics	Crib (42½″ × 62″)	Twin (84½″ × 93½″)	Queen (89″ × 97″)	King (112½″ × 97″)
Row layout*	39 strips × 2 wide rows and 80 strips × 1 narrow row	57 strips × 3 wide rows and 116 strips × 4 narrow rows	59 strips × 4 wide rows and 120 strips × 3 narrow rows	59 strips × 5 wide rows and 120 strips × 4 narrow rows
Blue/green prints	2½ yards total	4½ yards total	5⅞ yards total	7 yards total
White	¾ yard total	3 yards total	2⅜ yards total	3⅛ yards total
Black	⅞ yard	2¼ yards	2 yards	2⅜ yards
Backing	2¾ yards	7½ yards	8 yards	8¾ yards
Batting	49″ × 68″	90″ × 100″	95″ × 103″	118″ × 103″
Binding	½ yard	⅞ yard	⅞ yard	1 yard

This is the exact number of strips needed for each size layout, but it is useful to cut extras so you have some to play with.

CUTTING

Make templates using the side wedge E and F patterns (page 122).

Fabric*	Strip Size	Crib	Twin	Queen	King
Blue/green prints	3˝ × 10½˝	78	171	236	295
White I	1¾˝ × 6½˝	27	156	120	160
White II	1¾˝ × 7¾˝	26	152	120	160
Black I	1¾˝ × 6½˝	13	76	60	80
Black II	1¾˝ × 7¾˝	14	80	60	80
Black	Side Wedge E	19	28	29	29
Black	Side Wedge F	18	27	28	28

This is the exact number of strips needed for each size layout, but it is useful to cut extras so you have some to play with.

Construct the Blue/Green Rows

The approximate finished row width is 14˝ for the wide colored rows.

These wide rows are multicolored but are generally arranged with 2 light strips on each side of the row, then 1 dark strip on each side. Lay out the strips as desired, using the photo as a reference.

1. Follow the directions for Parlor Trick One: Partial-Seam Construction (page 13).

2. Sew the rows needed for your desired layout. Start at the bottom of each row with a strip on the left for the first 2 rows; then start with a strip on the right for the last 2 rows. (See Row Layout, page 37.)

NOTE > When the rows are put together, they don't line up straight horizontally because they are different widths. If all the rows are constructed starting with the same side strip, they will "step down" in small increments. Starting with a strip on the opposite side for two of the rows will fix this. Don't worry if you forget to do this; you will just need to add extra strips to the top or trim the quilt at a lower point.

Construct the Narrow White/Black Rows

The approximate finished row width is 9⅜˝. Press all seam allowances open if using black and white.

1. With right sides together and the ends aligned, sew the short end of a black I strip to the side of a white I strip, forming an L. *Fig. A*

A.

2. Flip open and press (or finger-press) the seam allowance open. *Fig. B*

B.

3. With right sides together and the top ends aligned, sew a white II strip to the left/top side of the unit. Sew across the entire seam. *Fig. C*

C.

4. Flip open and press the seam allowance open. *Fig. D*

5. In the same way as Steps 3 and 4, sew a black II strip to the right/top side of the unit. Sew all the way across this strip. *Fig. E*

6. Sew a white I strip to the left/top side. About 2″ from the outside edge of the strip being added, stop sewing and do a short backstitch to secure, creating a partial seam. *Fig. F*

7. Sew a white I strip to the right/top side. Again, stop and backstitch about 2″ from the outside edge.

8. Sew a black II strip to the left/top side.

9. Sew a white II strip to the right/top side.

10. Continue adding strips until the row reaches the number of strips needed for the desired layout. Alternate 2 white strips, then 1 black. When adding white II or black II strips, sew the whole seam. When adding white I or black I strips, stop and backstitch about 2″ from the outside edge. Press the seam allowances open. *Figs. G–O*

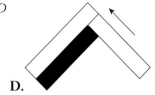

D.

E.

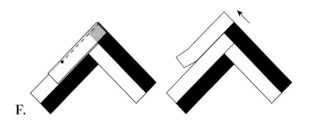

F.

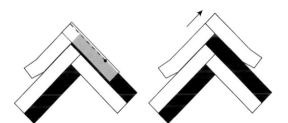

G. Add white I with partial seam; flip open and press seam allowances open.

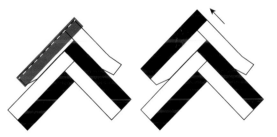

H. Add black II; flip open and press seam allowances open.

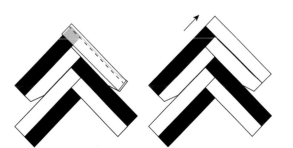

I. Add white II; flip open and press seam allowances open.

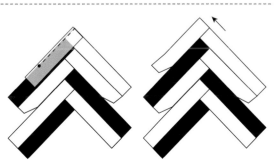

J. Add white I with partial seam; flip open and press seam allowances open.

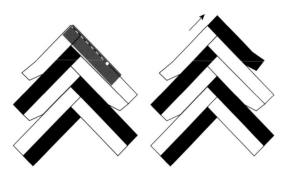

K. Add black I with partial seam; flip open and press seam allowances open.

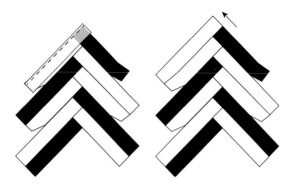

L. Add white II; flip open and press seam allowances open.

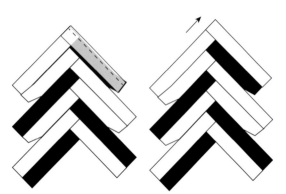

M. Add white II; flip open and press seam allowances open.

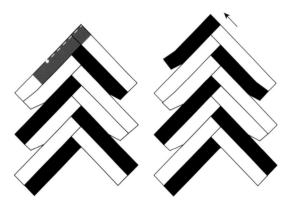

N. Add black I with partial seam; flip open and press seam allowances open.

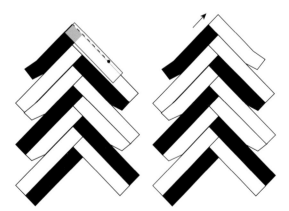

O. Add white I with partial seam; flip open and press seam allowances open.

11. Sew the remaining rows needed for your desired layout. Start at the bottom of each row with a strip on the left each time. Rows don't have to start with the same black I strip. Wherever you start, follow the established white/black pattern and short/long layout. *Fig. P*

P.

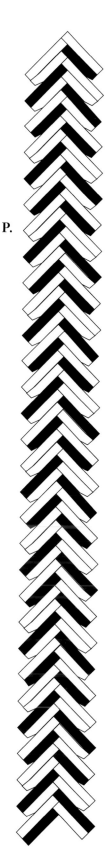

Row Layout

Arrange the rows in layout order. On the 2 outside wide rows, add wedge-shaped pieces (pattern pieces E and F) to finish the sides of the quilt with a straight edge.

1. With right sides together and the ends aligned, sew a piece F end to end with each strip on the left outside edge. *Fig. A*

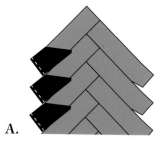

A.

2. Finger-press the seam allowances toward the outside. Starting from the top of the row, finish sewing the partial seams on that side. Press lightly. *Fig. B*

B.

3. Continue sewing pieces E to strips on the right outside edge. Then finish sewing the partial seams on that side. Sew an additional piece E to the top of the right side to fill in the corner. Press lightly. *Fig. C*

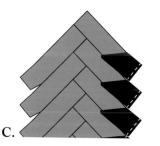

C.

Join the Rows

Working from the *top* of the rows *down*, join and complete the partial seams.

Refer to *Lavender Walls* (page 19) for instructions on joining the rows.

Follow the row layout diagram (at right) for the exact position and starting point of each row.

Row layout for queen-size quilt

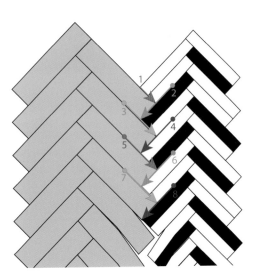

Finishing

1. Lightly press the quilt top, being careful not to stretch the fabrics.

2. Trim the top and bottom edges even with the innermost points.

3. Layer, quilt, and bind.

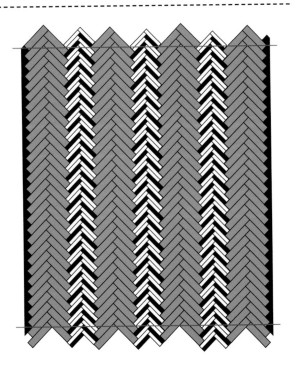

ENOUGH

Finished quilt: 100˝ × 100˝ (before quilting)

By Victoria Findlay Wolfe, quilted by Shelly Pagliai, 2016

Speaking of changing directions, I love four-block quilts! I make them with nearly every quilt design I touch. After playing with *Marion Lane* (page 31) and the directional designs that were happening, I wondered if I could do the same with this pattern. And after looking at two Trip Around the World quilts made from double-knit polyester by my grandmother, Elda Wolfe, I decided my answer was yes. The results definitely make a big statement.

Thinking about coloring books and filling in shapes with color allows me to change the story of the pattern. By doing so in a very minuscule way— chain piecing a strip of the opposite color on each end and breaking it into a four-block–style quilt— this happened! I simply changed one element within the block to get a very exciting new design.

Double-Knit Red, White, and Blue, by Elda Wolfe, 1983, 74″ × 79″

MATERIALS

Red solids/tonals: 6½ yards total

White solid / white-on-white prints: 5½ yards

Backing: 9 yards

Batting: 106″ × 106″

Binding: 1 yard

CUTTING

Fabric	Cut size	Number to cut
Red	**A:** 3″ × 9½″	196
	B: 3″ × 1½″	380
	C: 3″ × 8″	16
	D: 3″ × 5½″	16
	E: 3″ × 3″	16
White	**F:** 3″ × 8½″	196
	G: 3″ × 1½″	196
	H: 3″ × 9½″	4

Double-Knit Red, White, and Blue, by Elda Wolfe, 1983, 74″ × 79″

Construction Notes

The finished block size is 50˝ × 50˝. Make 4 identical blocks to rotate around the center point, forming an X through the quilt. Use a ¼˝ seam allowance.

NOTE > If you are using a light and a dark color, press *all* seam allowances open.

Piece the Strips

1. Sew a white G strip to a red A strip along the 3˝ side. Make 196. *Fig. A*

A.

2. From 24 of these pieced A/G strips, measure from the white edge and trim *(fig. B)*:

  8 strips to 3˝ × 3˝ squares

  8 strips to 3˝ × 5½˝ strips

  8 strips to 3˝ × 8˝ strips

B.

3. Sew a red B strip to a white H strip along the 3˝ side. Make 4. *Fig. C*

C.

4. Sew 2 red B strips to a white F strip, 1 on each 3˝ end. Make 180. *Fig. D*

5. From 16 of these pieced F/B strips, measure from each end of the strip and cut *(fig. E)*:

  16 squares 3˝ × 3˝

  16 strips 3˝ × 5½˝

D.
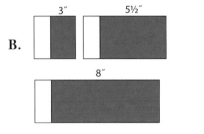

6. Sew a red B strip to a white F strip. Make 16.

7. Using these pieced strips, measure from the red edge and trim the strips to 3˝ × 8˝. *Fig. F*

E.

F.
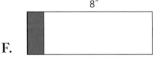

Block 1: Construct the Diagonal Rows

Work from the outside edge to build each row. Press lightly or finger-press the seam allowances open before the next intersecting seam.

Center Red Row

1. Sew 2 red E squares together.

2. Sew a red D strip to the long side, across the bottom of both squares.

3. Sew another red D strip to the right of this unit. *Fig. G*

G.

4. Sew a red C strip to the bottom, then sew another red C strip the right side of this unit. *Fig. H*

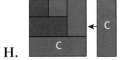

H.

5. Sew a pieced A/G strip to the bottom, with the white end on the left side. Then sew another A/G strip to the right side of this unit, with the white end at the top. *Fig. I*

6. Sew another A/G strip to the bottom, aligning the solid red ends. Sew to about 2″ before the end of the strip and secure with a short backstitch (partial seam).

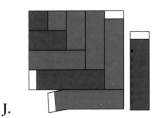

I.

7. Sew another A/G strip to the right side, aligning the solid red ends at the bottom of the piece. Sew to about 2″ before the end of the strip and secure with a short backstitch (partial seam). *Fig. J*

8. Repeat Steps 6 and 7 until there are 17 pieced A/G strips on the bottom and 16 pieced A/G strips on the right side. (These are all partial seams and the row ends with a bottom strip.) Set this diagonal row aside. *Fig. K*

J.

Left White Row

1. Sew the side of a 3″ × 3″ pieced white F/red B square to the end of a full-length pieced F/B strip, as shown. *Fig. L*

K.

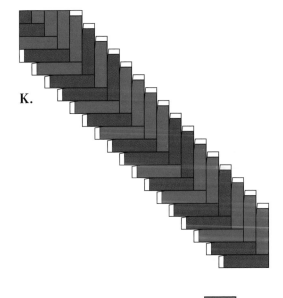

2. On the right edge, align another pieced F/B strip with the pieced square end. Start sewing from the pieced square end and sew to 2″ from the end of the new strip, securing with a short backstitch (partial seam). *Fig. M*

3. Sew the side of a 3″ × 5½″ pieced F/B strip to the bottom of this unit, with the red strip to the right. *Fig. N*

4. On the right edge, align another pieced F/B strip with the bottom rectangle. Start sewing from the bottom and sew to 2″ from the end of the new strip, securing with a short backstitch (partial seam).

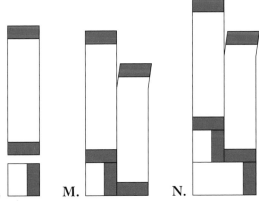

L.   M.   N.

5. Sew the side of a 3″ × 8″ pieced F/B strip to the bottom of this unit, with the red strip to the right. *Fig. O*

6. Repeat Step 4.

7. Sew a full-length pieced F/B strip to the bottom of this unit.

8. Repeat Step 4.

9. On the bottom edge, align another pieced F/B strip with the right side. Start sewing from the right side and sew to 2″ from the end of the new strip, securing with a short backstitch (partial seam).

10. Continue to alternate sewing pieced F/B strips on the right and bottom edges of your row, each time with a partial seam, until the row has 9 full-length F/B strips on the bottom and 12 full-length F/B strips on the right edge. *Fig. P*

11. Keeping the bottom edges even, align a pieced white H/red B strip to the right side with the red end at the top. Start sewing from the bottom edge, stopping 2″ before the end of this strip and securing with a short backstitch (partial seam).

12. In the same way, sew a trimmed 3″ × 8″ white F/red B strip, then a 3″ × 5½″ F/B strip, and finally a 3″ × 3″ F/B square. Set this diagonal row aside.

Right White Row

1. Sew the side of a 3″ × 3″ pieced white F/red B square to the end of a full-length pieced F/B strip, as shown.

2. On the bottom edge, align another pieced F/B strip with the pieced square end. Start sewing from the pieced square end and sew to 2″ from the end of the new strip, securing with a short backstitch (partial seam).

3. Sew the side of a 3″ × 5½″ pieced F/B strip to the right of this unit, with the red strip at the bottom.

4. On the bottom edge, align another pieced F/B strip with the pieced end. Start sewing from the right end and sew to 2″ from the end of the new strip, securing with a short backstitch (partial seam).

5. Sew the side of a 3″ × 8″ pieced F/B strip to the right of this unit, with the red strip at the bottom. *Fig. Q*

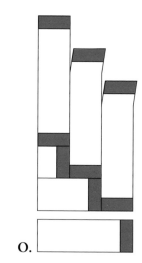

O.

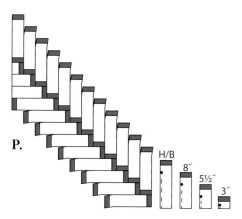

P.

H/B
8″
5½″
3″

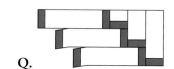

Q.

6. On the bottom edge, align another pieced F/B strip with the right end. Start sewing from the right end and sew to 2″ from the end of the new strip, securing with a short backstitch (partial seam).

7. Sew a full-length pieced F/B strip to the right of this unit.

8. On the bottom edge, align another pieced F/B strip with the right end. Start sewing from the right end and sew to 2″ from the end of the new strip, securing with a short backstitch (partial seam).

9. On the right edge, align another pieced F/B strip with the bottom rectangle. Start sewing from the bottom and sew to 2″ from the end of the new strip, securing with a short backstitch (partial seam).

10. Continue to alternate sewing pieced F/B strips on the bottom and right edges of your row, each time with a partial seam, until the row has 12 full-length F/B strips on the bottom and 8 full-length F/B strips on the right edge. *Fig. R*

R.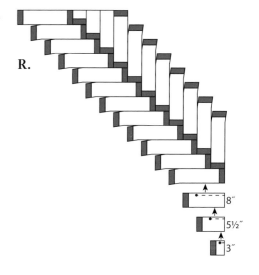

8″
5½″
3″

11. Keeping the right edges even, align a trimmed 3″ × 8″ white F/red B strip to the bottom side, with the red end at the left. Start sewing from the right edge, stopping 2″ before the end of this strip and securing with a short backstitch (partial seam).

12. In the same way, sew a trimmed 3″ × 5½″ white F/red B strip and then a 3″ × 3″ F/B square. Set this diagonal row aside.

Left Red Row

1. Sew a red E square to the bottom end of a pieced A/G strip. The white end of the A/G strip will be on top.

2. Sew an A/G strip to the right, aligning the solid red ends. Sew to about 2″ before the end of the new strip and secure with a short backstitch (partial seam).

3. Sew a red D strip to the bottom of this unit. *Fig. S*

S.

E

D

4. Sew another A/G strip to the right, aligning the solid red ends. Sew to about 2″ before the end of the new strip and secure with a short backstitch (partial seam).

5. Sew a red C strip to the bottom of this unit.

6. Sew an A/G strip to the right, aligning the solid red ends. Sew to about 2″ before the end of the new strip and secure with a short backstitch (partial seam).

7. Sew an A/G strip to the bottom of this unit, with the white end to the left.

8. Sew another A/G strip to the right, aligning the solid red ends. Sew to about 2″ before the end of the new strip and secure with a short backstitch (partial seam). *Fig. T*

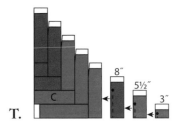

T.

9. Keeping the bottom edges even, align a trimmed 3″ × 8″ red A/white G strip to the right side, with the white end at the top. Start sewing from the bottom, stopping 2″ before the end of this strip and securing with a short backstitch (partial seam).

10. In the same way, sew a trimmed 3″ × 5½″ A/G strip and then a 3″ × 3″ A/G square. Set this diagonal row aside.

Right Red Row

1. Sew a red E square to the right end of a pieced A/G strip with the white end on the left side.

2. Sew a pieced A/G strip to the bottom, aligning the solid red ends. Sew to about 2″ before the end of the new strip and secure with a short backstitch (partial seam).

3. Sew a red D strip to the right of this unit. *Fig. U*

U.

4. Sew another A/G strip to the bottom, aligning the solid red ends. Sew to about 2″ before the end of the new strip and secure with a short backstitch (partial seam).

5. Sew a red C strip to the right of this unit.

6. Sew an A/G strip to the bottom, aligning the solid red ends. Sew to about 2″ before the end of the new strip and secure with a short backstitch (partial seam). *Fig. V*

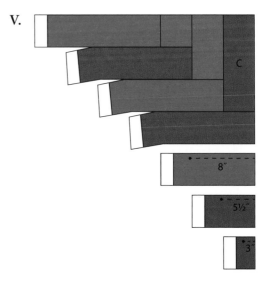

V.

7. Keeping the right edges even, align a trimmed 3″ × 8″ red A/white G strip to the bottom, with white end to the left. Start sewing from the right, stopping 2″ before the end of this strip and securing with a short backstitch (partial seam).

8. In the same way, sew a trimmed 3″ × 5½″ A/G strip and then a 3″ × 3″ A/G square.

Block 1: Joining the Rows

1. Starting from the lower right edge, sew the right red row to the right white row. Sew the end pieces together, then alternate down the row, finishing the partial seams as explained in Parlor Trick One: Partial-Seam Construction (page 13).

2. Starting from the bottom right edge, sew the left red row to the left white row in the same way.

3. Repeat to sew each side unit to the center red row.

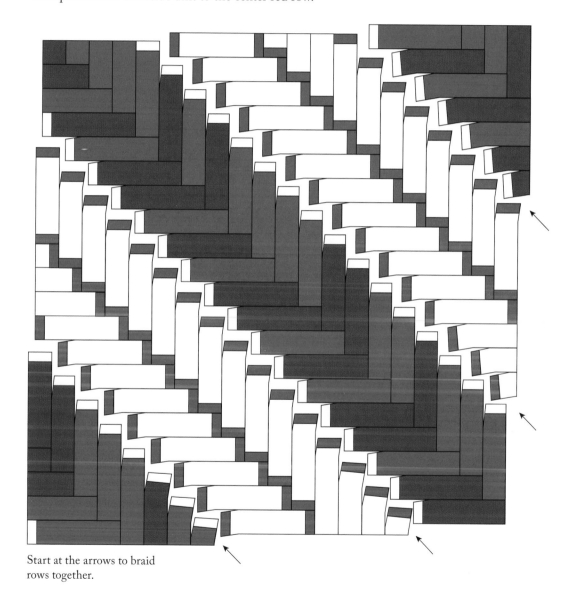

Start at the arrows to braid rows together.

Blocks 2, 3, and 4

Make 3 more identical blocks following the instructions for Block 1.

Final Assembly

1. Rotate the 4 blocks around the center, as shown. Sew the top 2 blocks together, pinning at each intersection to match seamlines. Sew the bottom 2 blocks together in the same way. Press the seam allowances open.

2. Sew the 2 halves together.

3. Layer, quilt, and bind.

Directionally Challenged, by Victoria Findlay Wolfe, 2015, 45˝ × 47˝

You can add improvisational piecing within the block. Here I used a neutral palette of whites and lights so the intricate piecing is evident, yet the focus is on the mini triangles floating precariously throughout the quilt.

You can adapt each or some of the rectangles' length and width as long as the size ultimately ends with the beginning block size.

This is a great place to look at negative space. How can you take information out of the design to disrupt the pattern? Sometimes taking out information is as important as putting it in. Less is more!

NEGATIVE SPACE,
POSITIVE ATTITUDE

Finished quilt: 80˝ × 90˝ (before quilting)

When I'm playing with a pattern, I like to see how else I can push the design. I often look at the horizontal and vertical lines within a quilt, and then I look to see how I can alter the pattern to make the directions change. So not only do I have horizontal and vertical lines, but I also have diagonal lines—all in one quilt! This is how the design of *Negative Space, Positive Attitude* came together.

When you first look at this quilt, you might think that it is strip pieced, or that it is a Log Cabin or Courthouse Steps. But it's not—the herringbone direction is simply changing left to right. The quilt is the same style as the partially seamed herringbone pattern. Instead of making one long row, I am breaking the row down into smaller sections, changing direction as I braid down the row. Historically, this is called a *coarse-woven block*.

I like that as a description, as it is indeed weaving the fabric in both directions.

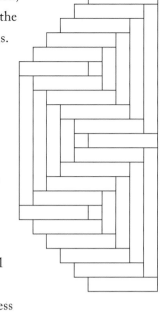

I am not only looking at the pattern but also at whether I can take information *out* of the quilt. How can I simplify the quilt to its bare bones to make a graphic statement? In this case, I made only two rows using colorful solids with black and white. I like the crispness of this quilt. It brought about a great conversation with Shelly about how we would plan the quilting.

By Victoria Findlay Wolfe, quilted by Shelly Pagliai, 2016

MATERIALS

White: 4 yards (Usable width must be at least 41″.)

White-on-white print: 1 yard

Black: ½ yard

Peach: ⅓ yard

Light pink: ⅓ yard

Pink: ⅓ yard

Light yellow: ⅓ yard

Straw: ¼ yard

Gold: ⅓ yard

Aqua: ⅓ yard

Blue: ⅓ yard

Gray blue: ⅓ yard

Backing: 7¼ yards

Batting: 86″ × 96″

Binding: ⅞ yard

CUTTING

Fabric	Cut size	Number to cut
White	90½″ × width of fabric	Subcut into 2 pieces 20½″ × 90½″
	A: 2½″ × 2½″	18
	B: 2½″ × 4½″	4
	D: 2½″ × 10½″	18
	F: 2½″ × 14½″	4
	G: 2½″ × 18½″	14
White-on-white print	A: 2½″ × 2½″	4
	C: 2½″ × 6½″	18
	E: 2½″ × 12½″	4
	F: 2½″ × 14½″	14
Black	2½″ × 10½″	18
Peach*	2½″ × 10½″	9
Light pink*	2½″ × 10½″	8
Pink*	2½″ × 10½″	9
Light yellow*	2½″ × 10½″	9
Straw*	2½″ × 10½″	6
Gold*	2½″ × 10½″	7
Aqua*	2½″ × 10½″	9
Blue*	2½″ × 10½″	7
Gray blue*	2½″ × 10½″	8

This is the exact number of strips needed for this layout, but it is useful to cut extras so you can play with color placement.

Construction Note

Finished row = 20˝ wide

Construct the Rows

Work from the *top* downward to construct these continuous coarse-woven rows.

1. Sew a white-on-white print A square to the end of a straw strip. Press toward the straw strip. Sew an aqua strip to the bottom, aligning with the white-on-white print end. Sew to about 2˝ before the end of the strip and secure with a short backstitch (partial seam). Press lightly toward the straw strip (only the part of the strip sewn). Sew a white B strip across the ends. Press the seam toward the aqua strip. *Fig. A*

2. Sew a white A square to the end of a black strip. Sew onto the bottom of the row. Press the seam toward the aqua strip. *Fig. B*

3. *Change the weave direction.* Sew a peach strip to the bottom, aligning with the white square end. Sew to about 2˝ before the end of the strip and secure with a short backstitch (partial seam). Press the seam allowances toward the black strip. Sew a white-on-white print C strip across the ends. Press the seam toward the white print strip. *Fig. C*

> **TIP** *If you've come to a seam you've mistakenly sewn all the way, don't panic—just loosen the end to "make" a partial seam.*

4. Finish sewing the partial seam below the straw strip. Press. Sew a gray-blue strip to the bottom, aligning with the white-on-white print end. Sew to about 2˝ before the end of the strip and secure with a short backstitch (partial seam). Press the seam toward the peach strip. *Fig. D*

5. Sew a white D strip across the right end. Press the seam toward the white strip. Sew a pink strip to the bottom, aligning with the white end. Sew to about 2˝ before the end of the strip and secure with a short backstitch (partial seam). Press the seam toward the gray-blue strip. *Fig. E*

6. Sew a white-on-white print E strip across the right end. Press the seam toward the white-on-white print strip. Sew a light yellow strip to the bottom, aligning with the white-on-white print end. Sew to about 2˝ before the end of the strip and secure with a short backstitch (partial seam). Press the seam toward the pink strip. *Fig. F*

7. Sew a white F strip across the right end. Press the seam toward the white strip. Sew a white A square to the end of a black strip. Sew onto the bottom of the row. Press the seam toward the light yellow strip. *Fig. G*

8. *Change the weave direction.* Sew a light pink strip to the bottom, aligning with the white square end. Sew to about 2˝ before the end of the strip and secure with a short backstitch (partial seam). Press toward the black strip. Sew a white-on-white print C strip across the ends. Press the seam toward the white square. *Fig. H*

9. Finish sewing the partial seam below the pink strip. Press. Sew a peach strip to the bottom, aligning with the white-on-white print end. Sew to about 2˝ before the end of the strip and secure with a short backstitch (partial seam). Press toward the light pink strip. *Fig. I*

10. Sew a white D strip across the left end. Press the seam toward the white-on-white print C strip. *Fig. J*

11. Finish sewing the partial seam below the gray-blue strip. Press. Sew a blue strip to the bottom, aligning with the white end. Sew to about 2″ before the end of the strip and secure with a short backstitch (partial seam). Press the seam toward the peach strip. *Fig. K*

12. Sew a white-on-white print F strip across the left end. Press the seam toward the white D strip. *Fig. L*

13. Finish sewing the partial seam below the peach strip. Press. Sew a gold strip to the bottom, aligning with the white-on-white print end. Sew to about 2″ before the end of the strip and secure with a short backstitch (partial seam). Press the seam toward the blue strip. *Fig. M*

14. Sew a white G strip across the left end. Press the seam toward the white-on-white print F strip. *Fig. N*

15. Sew a white A square to the end of a black strip. Sew onto the bottom of the row. Press the seam toward the gold strip. *Fig. O*

A.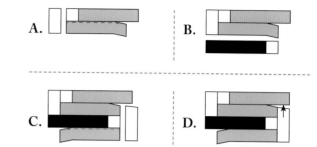

B.

C.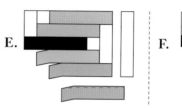

D.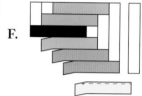

E.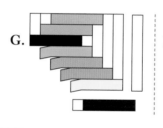

F.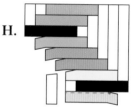

G.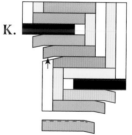

H.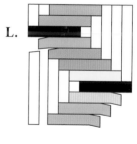

I.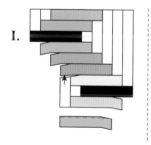

J.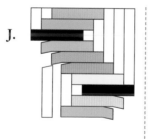

K.

L.

M.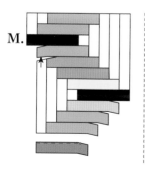

N.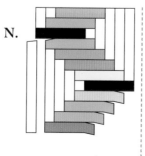

O.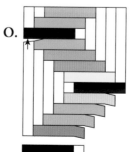

16. *Change the weave direction.* Continue sewing strips together this way, following the row 1 layout diagram for color placement and the strip length used. *Fig. P*

17. Sew the strips for row 2. Row 2 is a mirror-image version of row 1. The same construction steps apply, only it starts weaving to the right first rather than to the left. Follow the illustrations to get started and the row 2 layout diagram for color placement and the strip length used. *Figs. Q–V*

Join the Rows

1. Pin at each intersection to match the seams. Sew the 2 rows together on the long straight seam. *Fig. W*

2. Fold the 20½″ × 90½″ white pieces in fourths, finger-pressing on one long edge to mark the center and quarters. Do the same to the pieced rows. Pin a white piece on one long side of the center rows, matching the ends, centers, and quarter marks. Sew this seam. Then repeat with the other white piece on the opposite side of the pieced rows. Press the seam allowances.

Finishing

1. Lightly press the quilt top, being careful not to stretch the fabrics.

2. Layer, quilt, and bind.

P. Row 1 layout

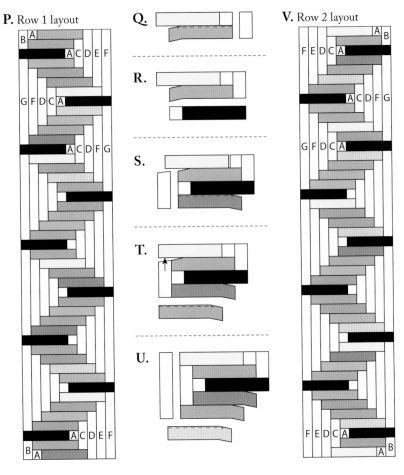

Q.

R.

S.

T.

U.

V. Row 2 layout

W.

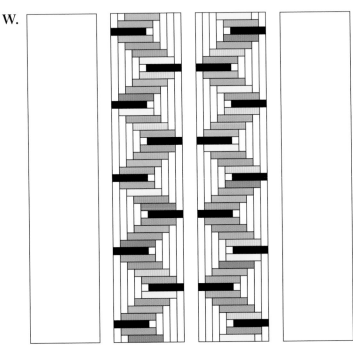

THE HAPPY WANDERER

Finished quilt: 80˝ × 90˝ (before quilting)

By Victoria Findlay Wolfe, quilted by Shelly Pagliai, 2016

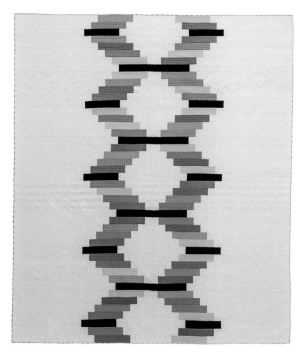

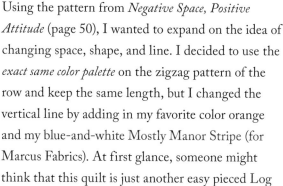

Using the pattern from *Negative Space, Positive Attitude* (page 50), I wanted to expand on the idea of changing space, shape, and line. I decided to use the *exact same color palette* on the zigzag pattern of the row and keep the same length, but I changed the vertical line by adding in my favorite color orange and my blue-and-white Mostly Manor Stripe (for Marcus Fabrics). At first glance, someone might think that this quilt is just another easy pieced Log

Cabin version; upon closer inspection, it truly looks like a quilt to boggle the mind. Layers—I love that! The more the better. By adding two more rows, I can change the scale and quietness into a busy map of color, pattern, and line.

It is quite interesting to look at *Negative Space, Positive Attitude* and *The Happy Wanderer* side by side to see how one little change in color placement totally changes the feel of this quilt.

MATERIALS

Orange: 2¼ yards

Blue-and-white stripe: 2¼ yards

Black: 1 yard

Peach: ⅝ yard

Light pink: ½ yard

Pink: ½ yard

Light yellow: ½ yard

Straw: ⅜ yard

Gold: ½ yard

Aqua: ½ yard

Blue: ½ yard

Gray blue: ½ yard

Backing: 7¼ yards

Batting: 86″ × 96″

Binding: ⅞ yard

CUTTING

Fabric	Cut size	Number to cut
Orange	**A:** 2½″ × 2½″	22
	B: 2½″ × 4½″	4
	C: 2½″ × 6½″	18
	D: 2½″ × 10½″	18
	E: 2½″ × 12½″	4
	F: 2½″ × 14½″	18
	G: 2½″ × 18½″	14
Blue-and-white stripe	**A:** 2½″ × 2½″	22
	B: 2½″ × 4½″	4
	C: 2½″ × 6½″	18
	D: 2½″ × 10½″	18
	E: 2½″ × 12½″	4
	F: 2½″ × 14½″	18
	G: 2½″ × 18½″	14
Black	2½″ × 10½″	36
Peach*	2½″ × 10½″	19
Light pink*	2½″ × 10½″	18
Pink*	2½″ × 10½″	18
Light yellow*	2½″ × 10½″	17
Straw*	2½″ × 10½″	12
Gold*	2½″ × 10½″	15
Aqua*	2½″ × 10½″	17
Blue*	2½″ × 10½″	14
Gray blue*	2½″ × 10½″	14

This is the exact number of strips needed for this layout, but it is useful to cut extras so you can play with color placement.

Construction Note

Finished row = 20″ wide

Construct the Rows

Work from the *top* downward to construct these continuous coarse-woven rows.

1. Follow the row assembly diagram for direction and color placement, and refer to *Negative Space, Positive Attitude*, Construct the Rows (page 54) for instructions. Rows 1 and 3 are the same as Row 2 in *Negative Space, Positive Attitude*; Rows 2 and 4 are the same as Row 1 in that quilt.

Row 1   Row 2   Row 3   Row 4

Row assembly

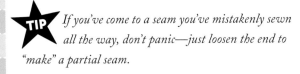

TIP *If you've come to a seam you've mistakenly sewn all the way, don't panic—just loosen the end to "make" a partial seam.*

Join the Rows

Pin at each intersection to match the seams. Sew the rows together in pairs on the long straight seam. Sew the pairs together.

Finishing

1. Lightly press the quilt top, being careful not to stretch the fabrics.

2. Layer, quilt, and bind.

Blocks

Partial-seam blocks are a great way to master partial seams! You could use these blocks on their own, or you could drop them into a herringbone quilt! (See *Mindful Balance*, page 71.) All blocks finish at 9″ × 9″.

Bright Hopes
block

Flower Star
block

Geese Squared block and Geese
Squared Pinwheel Variation block

Lacy Latticework
block

Double Star
block

Diamond Point
block

BRIGHT HOPES BLOCK

CUTTING

- Cut 1 square 3½″ × 3½″ for the center square.

- Cut 4 rectangles 3½″ × 6½″.

CONSTRUCTION

1. Place the square on the end of 1 rectangle, right sides together. Begin sewing these pieces together along the side. Stop halfway through the square and secure with a short backstitch. This is a partial seam. *Fig. A*

2. Flip open and press the seam allowance lightly toward the darker fabric.

3. Sew the next rectangle across the finished end of this unit. Press the seam allowances toward the rectangle. *Fig. B*

4. Continuing clockwise around the center square, sew the 2 remaining rectangles. Press the seam allowances toward the rectangle. When sewing the final rectangle, pull the first one (with the partial seam) slightly to the side and out of the way. Press.

5. Fold the first rectangle right sides together onto the block. Align the ends and finish the seam. Press. *Fig. C*

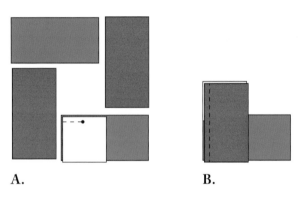

A.

B.

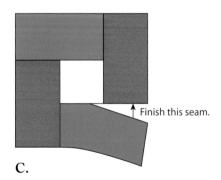

Finish this seam.

C.

FLOWER STAR BLOCK

CUTTING

- Cut 1 square 2½″ × 2½″ for the center square.

- Cut 4 using the Flower Star chisel shape pattern (page 123).

- Cut 4 using the Flower Star small triangle pattern (page 123).

CONSTRUCTION

1. With right sides together and following the dog-ears for alignment, sew each small triangle to a chisel shape. Press the seam allowances to the darker fabric. *Fig. A*

2. Arrange these rectangle units around the center square. Place the square on the end of 1 rectangle, right sides together. Begin sewing these pieces together along the side. Stop halfway through the square and secure with a short backstitch. This is a partial seam. *Fig. B*

3. Flip open and press the seam allowance lightly toward the darker fabric.

4. Finish sewing on the rectangular units and complete the partial seams. (See Bright Hopes Block, Steps 3–5, previous page).

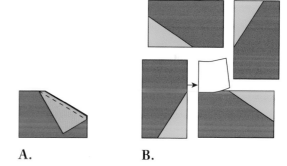

A.   **B.**

GEESE SQUARED BLOCK AND GEESE SQUARED PINWHEEL VARIATION BLOCK

Geese Squared block

Geese Squared Pinwheel Variation block

CUTTING

- Cut 1 square 3½″ × 3½″ for the center square.

- Cut 1 square 7¼″ × 7¼″; subcut in half diagonally in both directions to make 4 triangles for the geese triangles. *Fig. A*

- Cut 4 squares 3⅞″ × 3⅞″; subcut each in half diagonally to make 8 triangles for the small triangles. *Fig. B*

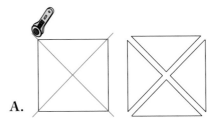

A.

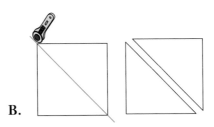

B.

CONSTRUCTION

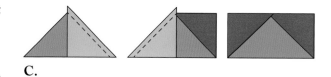

1. Sew the long edge of a small triangle to the short side of a geese triangle. Press the seam allowances to the darker fabric. In the same way, sew another small triangle to the other short side. Press. Repeat, making 4 rectangular Flying Geese units. *Fig. C*

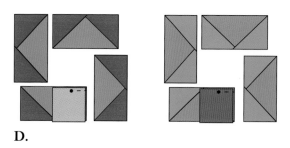

C.

2. Arrange these Flying Geese units around the center square, with the geese triangle points facing out for the Geese Squared block *or* the points facing inward for the Geese Squared Pinwheel Variation block. Place the square on the end of 1 rectangle, right sides together, pinning to match points at the center square. Begin sewing these pieces together along the side. Stop halfway through the square and secure with a short backstitch. This is a partial seam. *Fig. D*

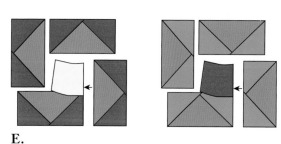

D.

3. Flip open and press the seam allowance lightly toward the darker fabric.

4. Sew the next rectangle across the finished end of this unit, pinning to match points. Press. *Fig. E*

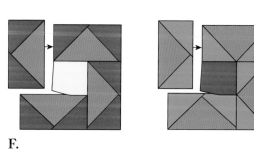

E.

5. Continuing counterclockwise around the center square, sew the 2 remaining rectangles, pinning to match the points. When sewing the final rectangle, pull the first one (with the partial seam) slightly to the side and out of the way. Press. *Fig. F*

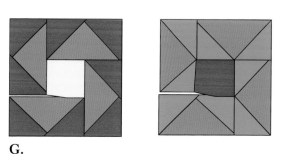

F.

6. Fold the first rectangle right sides together onto the block. Align the ends, pin to match the points, and finish the seam. Press. *Fig. G*

G.

LACY LATTICEWORK BLOCK

CUTTING

• Cut 1 square 2″ × 2″.

• Cut 4 rectangles 2″ × 5¾″.

• Cut 8 using the Lacy Latticework triangle
  pattern (page 123): 4 from fabric A and
  4 from fabric B.

CONSTRUCTION

1. With right sides together, sew each
triangle A to a triangle B on the long side. Press
the seam allowances to the darker fabric. *Fig. A*

2. Sew the long edge of a rectangle to the
bottom of each triangle unit. *Fig. B*

3. Arrange these rectangular units around the
center square. Place the square on the end of
1 rectangle, right sides together. Begin sewing
these pieces together along the side. Stop halfway through the square and secure with a short
backstitch. This is a partial seam. *Fig. C*

4. Finish sewing on the rectangular units and
complete the partial seams. (See Geese Squared
Block and Geese Squared Pinwheel Variation
Block, Steps 3–6, page 65).

A.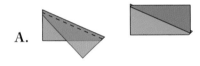

B.

C.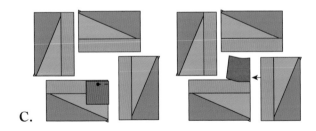

DOUBLE STAR BLOCK

CUTTING

- Cut 1 square 2″ × 2″.

- Cut 2 squares 4⅝″ × 4⅝″; subcut each in half diagonally to make 4 big triangles. *Fig. A*

- Cut 2 squares 5″ × 5″: 1 from fabric A and 1 from fabric B. Subcut in half diagonally in both directions to make 4 small triangles A and 4 small triangles B. *Fig. B*

- Cut 4 rectangles 2″ × 4¼″.

CONSTRUCTION

1. Sew each small triangle A to a small triangle B along one short side. Press the seam allowance to the darker fabric. *Fig. C*

2. Sew the long edge of each big triangle to an A/B triangle unit, forming a square. *Fig. D*

3. Sew a rectangle to the side adjacent to the small triangle A. Repeat on all 4 units. Press the seam allowances to the darker fabric. *Fig. E*

4. Arrange the rectangular units around the center square. Place the square on the end of 1 rectangle, right sides together. Begin sewing these pieces together along the side. Stop halfway through the square and secure with a short backstitch. This is a partial seam. *Fig. F*

5. Finish adding the rectangular units and complete the partial seam. (See Bright Hopes Block, Steps 2–5, page 62).

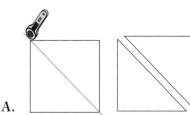

A.

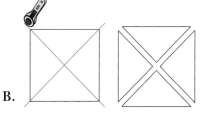

B.

C.   D.   E.

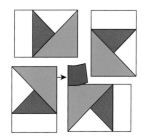

F.

DIAMOND POINT BLOCK

CUTTING

• Cut 1 square 4¼″ × 4¼″.

• Cut 16 using the Diamond Point diamond pattern (page 123): 4 from fabric A, 4 from fabric B, and 8 from fabric C.

• Cut 4 squares 3½″ × 3½″; subcut each in half diagonally to make 8 triangles. *Fig. A*

CONSTRUCTION

1. Arrange the pieces for the block. On each side of the square, sew the 2 diamonds closest to the center together. Sew the 2 diamonds on the outside edge together. Press the seam allowances open. *Fig. B*

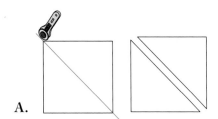

A.

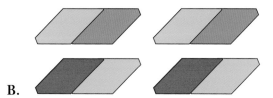

B.

2. Sew these 2 units together, creating a larger diamond. The center seams will intersect at the ¼″ seamline. *Fig. C*

3. Sew the long side of a triangle to the opposite sides of each large diamond. *Fig. D*

4. Arrange these rectangular units around the center square. Place the square on the end of 1 rectangle, right sides together. Begin sewing these pieces together along the side. Stop half-way through the square and secure with a short backstitch. This is a partial seam. *Fig. E*

5. Finish sewing on the rectangular units and complete the partial seam. (See Geese Squared Block and Geese Squared Pinwheel Variation Block, Steps 3–6, page 65).

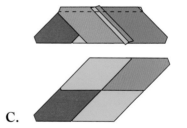
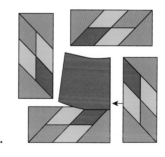

C.

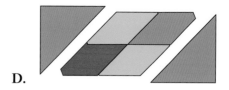

D.

E.

CLASS PROJECT: PARLOR-TRICK BABY QUILT

These swirly partial-seam blocks are fun to play with for a lap or baby quilt. See Parlor Trick Two: Blocks with Partial Seams (page 61) for instructions on making each one. Then add various 9½″ × 9½″ squares of scrappy fabrics to fill in between blocks and make your own design! Keep it simple, and spend time mastering your partial seams.

As illustrated, the quilt is 45″ × 45″.

MATERIALS

2 Bright Hopes blocks (page 62)

2 Flower Star blocks (page 63)

1 Geese Squared block (page 64)

2 Geese Squared Pinwheel Variation blocks (page 64)

2 Lacy Latticework blocks (page 66)

2 Double Star blocks (page 67)

2 Diamond Point blocks (page 68)

Fabric: 12 alternate squares 9½″ × 9½″ *or* 1⅛ yards of 1 fabric

Backing: 3 yards

Batting: 51″ × 51″

Binding: ½ yard

Construct the Quilt

1. Arrange the blocks in a 5 × 5 grid.

2. Sew the blocks together into rows, pressing the seams toward the alternate squares.

3. Sew the rows together, matching the seams.

4. Press the seams in one direction.

Finishing

1. Lightly press the quilt top, being careful not to stretch the fabrics.

2. Layer, quilt, and bind.

MINDFUL BALANCE

Finished quilt: 102½˝ × 91½˝ (before quilting)

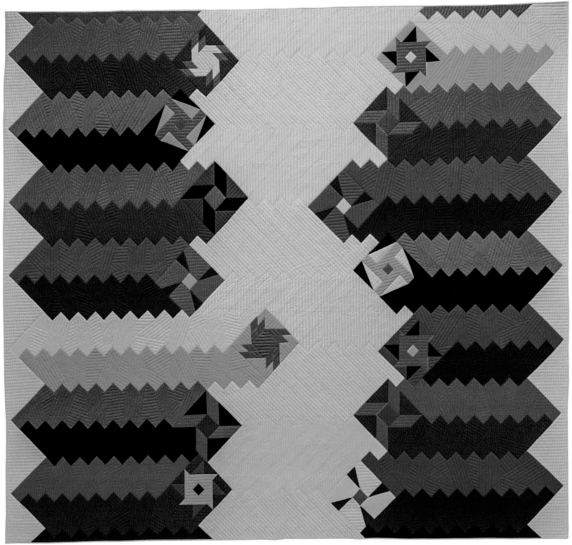

By Victoria Findlay Wolfe, quilted by Frank Palmer, 2016

Use the herringbone concept from Parlor Trick One (page 13) and add partial-seam blocks for a spiral effect, over-the-top movement, and dimension!

MATERIALS

Buff: 3½ yards

Hot pink: 1¾ yards

Faded plum: 1½ yards

Steel blue: 1 yard

Navy: 1¼ yards

Teal: 1½ yards

Dark teal: 1⅛ yards

Lime: ¾ yard

Aqua: 1 yard

Backing: 8¼ yards

Batting: 109″ × 98″

Binding: 1 yard

CUTTING

Make templates with Mindful Balance patterns N, O, and P (page 124).

Fabric	Cut size	Number to cut
Buff	2¾″ × 9½″	94
	2¾″ × 7¼″	14
	2¾″ × 5″	14
	2¾″ × 2¾″	14
	Template N	9
	Template P	13
	15″ × 15″	4 squares 15″ × 15″, subcut in half diagonally in both directions to make 16 triangles
Hot pink	2¾″ × 9½″	45
Faded plum	2¾″ × 9½″	44
Steel blue	2¾″ × 9½″	26
	Template N	6
Navy	2¾″ × 9½″	25
	Template N	10
Teal	2¾″ × 9½″	37
	Template O	1
	Template P	9
Dark teal	2¾″ × 9½″	33
	Template O	1
	Template P	9
Lime	2¾″ × 9½″	20
Aqua	2¾″ × 9½″	19

Make the Blocks

Follow Parlor Trick Two: Blocks with Partial Seams (page 61) to make 14 blocks.

Flower Star blocks

Geese Squared blocks. Make 2 of first block.

Double Star blocks

Lacy Latticework blocks. Second block is a mirror-image layout.

Diamond Point blocks

Construct the Rows

The approximate finished row height is 12½˝. Rows are constructed starting from each block. Fig. A

1. Beginning with the bottom left block, alternate partially seaming first a faded plum strip, then a hot pink strip—repeating until you have 9 strips of each color. Stop sewing about 2˝ from the outside end of each strip, securing with a short backstitch. For more detailed instructions, refer to Parlor Trick One: Partial-Seam Construction (page 13). Press all the seam allowances away from the block. *Fig. B*

2. With the bottom right block, alternate partially seaming first a teal strip, then a dark teal strip—repeating until there are 10 teal strips and 9 dark teal strips. Stop sewing about 2˝ from the outside end of each strip, securing with a short backstitch. Press all the seam allowances away from the block.

3. On the other 2 sides of the bottom right block, alternate partially seaming buff strips to the top and then the bottom—repeating until you have 12 strips sewn (6 on the top and 6 on the bottom). Stop sewing about 2˝ from the outside end of each strip, securing with a short backstitch. Press all the seam allowances away from the block.

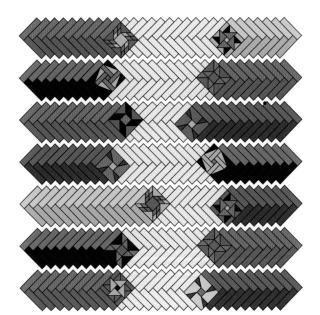

A. Row layout

4. Keeping the top edges aligned, continue sewing: add first a buff 2¾˝ × 7¼˝ strip, leaving the last 2˝ on the outside edge free; then partial seam a 2¾˝ × 5˝ strip; and finally a 2¾˝ × 2¾˝ square. Press all the seam allowances away from the block. *Fig. C*

5. Keeping the bottom ends aligned, partially seam a buff 2¾″ × 2¾″ square to a 2¾″ × 5″ strip and a 2¾″ × 7¼″ strip, each time leaving about 2″ on the outside (uneven) edge free. Press all the seam allowances toward the square.

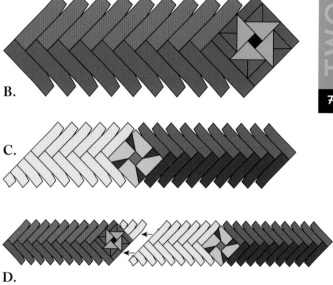

B.

6. Sew the even ends of this unit to the left block as shown, leaving about 2″ of the 2¾″ square free. Press all the seam allowances away from the block. Pin, matching the intersecting seam; then sew the diagonal seam to join the left and right parts of the row. The bottom buff square should overlap the intersecting seam by ¼″. Start and stop this seam about 2″ from the end of the shortest pieces. Press the seam allowance to one side. *Fig. D*

C.

D.

7. Using the row layout diagram (previous page), build the colored sections of each row, starting with a block. Then complete the rows as in Steps 1–6, noting the direction of the buff strips and the number of strips needed.

Side Setting Triangles

1. Pin the short side of 1 triangle along the side of a row's top outside strip, aligning the point of the triangle with the inside point of the row. The outside edge of the triangle will overlap significantly. Pin the fabric as it lies, being careful not to stretch the fabric; then sew. Press the seam allowance toward the triangle.

2. Repeat Step 1, sewing a triangle on the top end strip of each row. These will be sewn between the rows to straighten the quilt sides. Trim the bottom side of the triangle even with the edge of the row, as shown. *Fig. E*

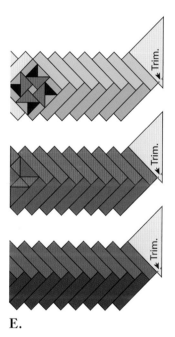

E.

Row Layout

1. After completing the rows, finalize the row layout order. On the top and bottom rows, add wedge- and triangle-shaped pieces—Mindful Balance top/bottom wedge N, triangle edge piece O, and top/bottom wedge P patterns (page 124)—to finish the edges of the quilt with a straight edge. (See the diagrams for the color placement and direction of each piece.)

2. With right sides together and the ends aligned, sew the buff wedge pieces end to end, with each strip on the top outside edge. Finger-press the seam allowances toward the outside. Finish sewing the partial seams. Press lightly.

3. Starting at each outside edge of the quilt, sew a colored wedge-shaped piece to the side of the strip. Then finish sewing the partial seam on that side. Press lightly. Continue to the middle of the quilt. Finish with the triangle O piece. *Figs. F & G*

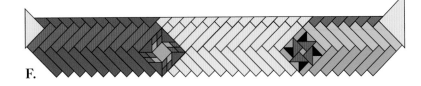

F.

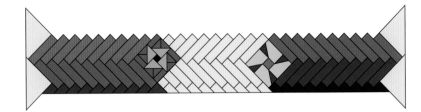

G.

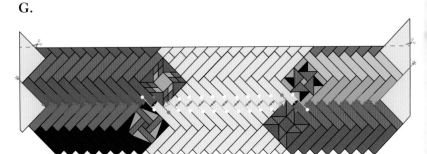

H. Joining rows

Join the Rows

 *This herringbone goes beyond the basics by changing direction mid-row, making joining the rows seem a little trickier. If you've come to a seam you've mistakenly sewn all the way, don't panic—just loosen the end to "make" a partial seam.*

1. See the joining rows diagram for sewing the rows and completing partial seams. Start with the side setting triangle between 2 adjacent rows. Align the free short side of the setting triangle to the bottom edge strip of the row above. Be careful not to stretch as you sew to attach the triangle to the next row and start sewing the rows together. Press the seams to one side.

2. Work from the outside of the rows inward, joining and completing the partial seams. (See Parlor Trick One: Partial-Seam Construction, page 13,

for more detailed instructions.) Continue until you reach a block, indicated by the blue arrows. *Fig. H*

3. Sew the ends of the buff strips going the same direction together, as indicated by the red arrows. Press the seam allowances to one side.

4. Complete the partial seams between same-direction strips, as indicated by the white lines. Press the seam allowances to one side.

5. Finally, complete the partial seams remaining by the blocks, as indicated by the green arrows first, then the green lines. Press the seam allowances to one side.

Finishing

1. Trim the corner triangles to be even with the top and bottom quilt edges. Lightly press the quilt top, being careful not to stretch the fabrics.

2. Layer, quilt, and bind.

PARLOR TRICK THREE:
MINI MADE FABRIC

Miniature Play

At the beginning of all my Fifteen Minutes of Play classes, I talk about process and play, and then I show the many samples of how play can manifest itself in one's work. At the very end of the class, I show three mini quilts using the mini made-fabric technique. Gasps, oohs, and aahs fill the room, and I share with my students that they already know how to do this. Many are skeptical and can't figure out how to sew all those tiny pieces together.

I say, "I call this my parlor trick. You learn this little technique, go home, make a quilt, and impress all your friends who know nothing about quiltmaking. They will be throwing compliments at you left and right about your fabulous skills!" This is where I remind them to just say, "Why, thank you so much!" The options are limitless for these little cuties!

Using up scraps is very satisfying. Generally I use solids because they show off the pieces better than prints (and are downright adorable). Just make a few each day, throw them into a mason jar, and watch the jar fill up.

Go ahead; I dare you.... Give it a try!

You won't be able to stop at one. (Just like potato chips!) Before you know it, you'll have made ten. And *please* don't forget ... when you finish your king-size quilt, send pictures!

MATERIALS

I save my smaller solid scraps and put them in a plastic bag to use for my minis—not itty-bitty pieces, but manageable pieces approximately 2″ × 3″.

CONSTRUCTION

1. Begin with an approximate 1″ × 1″ wonky, 5-sided, and house-shaped solid scrap. This is the smallest piece I use. *Fig. A*

2. Place another solid scrap, right sides together, over the bottom edge of the house shape, overlapping on both sides. Sew together with a seam allowance larger than ¼″. By doing so, your "house" will get smaller and smaller as you work around the shape. Trim the seam allowance to ⅛″. *Fig. B*

3. Flip the seam open; press it toward the outside. Working counter-clockwise (or clockwise—it doesn't matter the direction as long as the pieces are added in a continuous order), trim to form a straight edge for the next seam. Use the right side of your house shape as a guide. *Fig. C*

NOTE > The trick is sewing with a wide seam allowance. This makes your shapes get smaller and smaller to fit in your 1½″ template.

4. Place a longer solid scrap right sides together over this edge, over-lapping on both sides. Sew across (always with a wide seam allowance), trim the seam allowance to ⅛″, and press as in Step 3. *Fig. D*

5. Trim to form a straight edge for the next seam. *Fig. E*

6. Repeat Steps 2–5 for the remaining 3 sides.

7. Place your 1½″ template (or acrylic ruler) over the piece as desired and trim. *Fig. F*

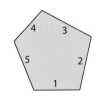

A.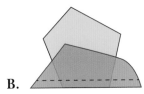

B.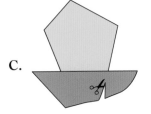

C.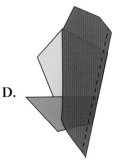

D.

E.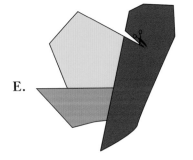

F.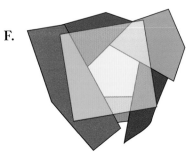

Trim to 1½″ × 1½″ square.

CLASS PROJECT: MINI QUILT 1

By Victoria Findlay Wolfe, 2013, 12″ × 12″

MATERIALS

16 made-fabric 1½″ × 1½″ squares from Miniature Play (page 77)

Inner border: 1 fat quarter

Outer border: 1 fat quarter

Backing: 14″ × 14″

Batting: 14″ × 14″

Binding: ¼ yard (2 strips 2½″ × width of fabric)

CUTTING

Inner border

- Cut 2 rectangles 3″ × 4½″.

- Cut 2 rectangles 3″ × 9½″.

Outer border

- Cut 2 rectangles 2″ × 9½″.

- Cut 2 rectangles 2″ × 12½″.

Construction

1. Make 16 made-fabric minis following Parlor Trick Three: Mini Made Fabric (page 77).

2. Sew together in rows of 4. Press the seam allowances open. Pin at each intersection and sew the rows together, forming a sixteen-patch. Press the seam allowances open.

3. Sew the 3″ × 4½″ rectangles onto opposite sides of the sixteen-patch, along the 4½″ sides. Press the seam allowances outward. Sew the inner border 3″ × 9½″ rectangles onto the other 2 sides, pressing the seam allowances outward.

4. Sew the outer border 2″ × 9½″ rectangles to opposite sides; then sew the 2″ × 12½″ rectangles onto the other 2 sides, pressing the seam allowances outward.

Finishing

1. Lightly press the quilt top, being careful not to stretch the fabrics.

2. Layer, quilt, and bind.

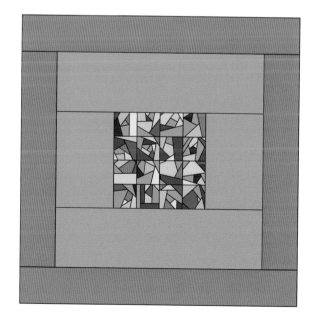

CLASS PROJECT: MINI QUILT 2

By Victoria Findlay Wolfe, 2013, 12″ × 12″

MATERIALS

9 made-fabric 1½″ × 1½″ squares from Miniature Play (page 77)

Star points and inner border: 1 fat quarter

Star setting: 1 fat quarter

Outer border: 1 fat quarter

Backing: 14″ × 14″

Batting: 14″ × 14″

Binding: ¼ yard *or* 2 strips 2½″ × width of fabric

CUTTING

Star points
- Cut 8 squares 2″ × 2″.

Star setting
- Cut 4 rectangles 2″ × 3½″.
- Cut 4 squares 2″ × 2″.

Inner border
- Cut 2 rectangles 1″ × 6½″.
- Cut 2 rectangles 1″ × 7½″.

Outer border
- Cut 2 rectangles 3″ × 7½″.
- Cut 2 rectangles 3″ × 12½″.

Construction

1. Make 9 made-fabric minis, following Parlor Trick Three: Mini Made Fabric (page 77).

2. Sew together in rows of 3. Press the seam allowances open. Pin at each intersection and sew the rows together, forming a nine-patch. Press the seam allowances open.

3. Draw a diagonal line on the back of the 8 squares 2″ × 2″. Place 1 right sides together on the end of a star setting 2″ × 3½″ rectangle. Sew on the diagonal line. Trim ¼″ outside the line, cutting off the small triangles. Press the seam allowances to the darker fabric.

4. Repeat with another 2″ square on the other end of the rectangle, with the diagonal line pointing in the opposite direction.

5. Make 4 star point units following Steps 3 and 4. Sew 2 of these units to opposite sides of the mini nine-patch. Press the seam allowances outward.

6. Sew a star setting 2″ square to both ends of the remaining star point units. Press the seam allowances away from the squares. Sew these units to the remaining sides of the nine-patch, pinning to match the seams.

7. Sew the shorter inner borders onto opposite sides of the star. Press the seam allowances outward. Then sew the longer inner borders onto the other 2 sides, pressing the seam allowances outward.

8. Repeat Step 7 with the outer borders.

Finishing

1. Lightly press the quilt top, being careful not to stretch the fabrics.

2. Layer, quilt, and bind.

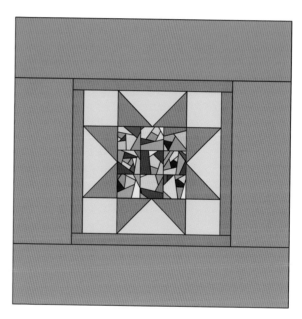

CLASS PROJECT: MINI QUILT 3

By Victoria Findlay Wolfe, 2013, 12″ × 12″

MATERIALS

20 made-fabric 1½″ × 1½″ squares from Miniature Play (page 77)

Center and setting triangles: 1 fat quarter

Border: 1 fat quarter

Backing: 14″ × 14″

Batting: 14″ × 14″

Binding: ¼ yard *or* 2 strips 2½″ × width of fabric

CUTTING

Center
• Cut 1 square 4½″ × 4½″.

Setting triangles
• Cut 2 squares 5⅛″ × 5⅛″; subcut in half diagonally to make 4 triangles.

Border
• Cut 2 rectangles 2¼″ × 9″.

• Cut 2 rectangles 2¼″ × 12½″.

Construction

1. Make 20 made-fabric minis, following Parlor Trick Three: Mini Made Fabric (page 77).

2. Sew together in 2 rows of 4. Press the seam allowances open. Sew the rows onto opposite sides of the center square. Press the seam allowances toward the center.

3. Sew the remaining minis in 2 rows of 6. Press the seam allowances open. Sew the rows onto the remaining sides of the center square. Press the seam allowances toward the center.

4. Sew the long edge of a setting triangle to opposite sides of the square. Press the seam allowances outward. Then sew the 2 remaining triangles to the other sides of the square.

5. Sew the shorter border rectangles to opposite sides; then sew the longer border rectangles onto the other 2 sides. Press the seam allowances outward.

Finishing

1. Lightly press the quilt top, being careful not to stretch the fabrics.

2. Layer, quilt, and bind.

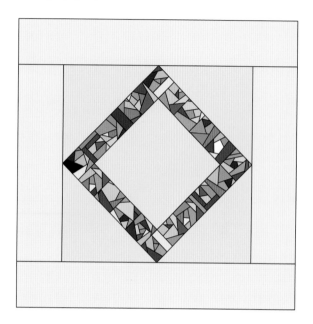

PARLOR TRICK FOUR:
Y-SEAMS

LeMoyne Star

Kick the words, "I am scared of Y-seams!" out of your quilter vocabulary! Whether you are a beginner or someone who has been quilting for years, Y-seams are not hard to learn. Why should fear hold you back on any of your creative adventures? What on earth do you have to lose? Take some scraps, learn the technique, and a plethora of new blocks are available to you! It literally takes fifteen minutes to learn this technique.

If you follow the order I recommend to put this block together, you will have success. I am sharing *two* tips you need to learn to make this block:

TIP 1 At any Y-seam, stop ¼″ before the end of the fabric. This allows for movement at your pivot point.

TIP 2 Follow the directions *exactly*, and you will always have a pressed-open seam on *top*, which helps you see where to leave your needle when pivoting at your Y-seam! *Look carefully* at the diagrams.

Learning to piece this block in four sections is one secret for success—go for it!

MATERIALS	CUTTING
Diamonds: 8 scraps 5″ × 10″	• Cut 8 using the LeMoyne Star diamond pattern (page 125).
Background: 1 fat quarter	• Cut 4 squares 4⅞″ × 4⅞″.
	• Cut 1 square 7½″ × 7½″; subcut in half diagonally in both directions to make 4 setting triangles. *Fig. A*

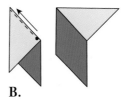

A.

CONSTRUCTION

1. With right sides together, sew 1 setting triangle to a diamond. Starting ¼″ from the edge of the fabric at the inner diamond point, backstitch and sew to the outside edge. Open and press the seam allowance open. *Fig. B*

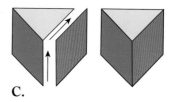

B.

2. Place the diamond/triangle piece on top of a second diamond star point, right sides together. Start sewing from the bottom point of the diamond. Stop sewing ¼″ from the inner corner (at the intersecting seam). With your needle in the down position, pivot at the corner, bringing the top of the diamond and the side of the triangle edges together. Continue sewing to the outer edge of the block. *Fig. C*

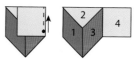

C.

3. Sew 1 setting square to the right-hand side of the second diamond. Start ¼″ from the inner corner of the square and sew the outer edge of the square. *Fig. D*

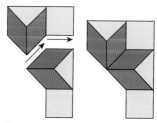

D. Quarter-star unit. Make 4.

4. Repeat Steps 1–3 with the remaining pieces to make 4 of these units.

5. Sew 2 quarter-star units together starting at the star center. With the needle in the down position at the inner corner, pivot with the fabric edges together to make a half-star unit. Make 2 half-star units. *Fig. E*

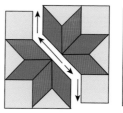

E. Half-star unit. Make 2.

6. Sew 2 half-star units together by pinning the center points of each half-star unit to align and by pinning the diamond sides together. Start sewing 2″ before the center point; sew through the center and continue to the outer edge. Flip the whole piece over. Beginning from the inside of the block, pin and complete the seam, pivoting at the corner as before to complete the star. *Fig. F*

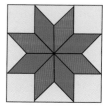

F.

CLASS PROJECT: LEMOYNE STAR PILLOW

By Victoria Findlay Wolfe, 2016, 20″ × 20″

Make a LeMoyne Star block from Parlor Trick Four: Y-Seams (page 84) and turn it into a pillow! Mastering this skill prepares you for the larger projects in this chapter.

MATERIALS

LeMoyne Star (page 84)

Border: ¼ yard

Muslin: ⅔ yard for pillow quilt backing

Batting: 22″ × 22″

Pillow backing: ⅔ yard

20″ pillow form

Binding: ⅓ yard

CUTTING

Border

• Cut 2 pieces 15½″ × 3″.

• Cut 2 border pieces 20½″ × 3″.

Muslin: Cut 1 square 22″ × 22″.

Pillow backing: Cut 2 rectangles 20½″ × 15″.

Pillow Finishing

1. Sew the long edges of the shorter border strips on opposite sides of the LeMoyne Star block. Sew the remaining border strips on the other 2 sides of the block. Press.

2. Layer the LeMoyne Star block, batting, and muslin.

3. Quilt.

4. Trim all layers even with the pieced top.

5. On one long edge of each pillow backing rectangle, press under ⅜″; then press under 3″. Top-stitch on both long sides of the 3″ section, close to the edge, creating a cleanly finished band. *Fig. A*

6. Place the *wrong* sides together with the front quilted panel. The back panels with the finished edges will overlap in the middle.

A.

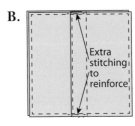

B.

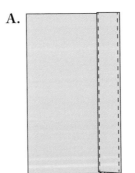

Extra stitching to reinforce

7. Sew around all 4 sides, pivoting in the corners to turn. I like to reinforce the edges on the sides where the back pieces overlap. In the seam allowance, add another line of stitching in the overlap areas. *Fig. B*

8. Cut the binding and apply it to the front, just as for a quilt. Fold around to the back and hand stitch down.

9. Insert a 20″ pillow form through the back overlap. It can be removed easily for cleaning.

SOIGNÉ

Finished quilt: 89˝ × 89˝ (before quilting)

By Victoria Findlay Wolfe, quilted by Shelly Pagliai, 2016

soigné \swän-'yā\ *adj* : carefully or elegantly done, operated, or designed

Putting most of the elements in this book together in one quilt is certainly one way to get the *wow* factor. I wanted a quilt that incorporated as many tricks as possible and used some eye-popping, modern color choices. I think this quilt hit the nail on the head! It has coarse-woven borders with Y-seam stars, braids running around the inner medallion, partial-seam blocks, and minis. And another big plus—it is also scrappy (my favorite look)!

I included my pink-and-red and gold-and-white Mostly Manor Stripe (for Marcus Fabrics).

Soigné was inspired by an earlier quilt of mine named *Polished Timber*. I was incorporating elements from an antique Log Cabin quilt to make a modern version. I trimmed the herringbone edges to a smooth braid to help with the visual layering effect within the quilt.

Polished Timber, by Victoria Findlay Wolfe, 2015, 58˝ × 58˝

Illustrated in the book *Log Cabin Fever*, International Quilt Study Center & Museum

---

MATERIALS

Aqua solid: 1 yard for center blocks and border stripes

Variety of aqua prints and solids: 2 yards total for background and border strips

Bright yellow solids and tonal prints: 1¾ yards for center block, on-point braid, and border squares

White solid: 1½ yards for center block, half-square triangles, on-point braid, stars, and border squares

Hot pink solid: ½ yard for center half-square triangles

Navy solid: 2½ yards for center block border, half-square triangles, stars, border stripes, and binding

Pink-and-red stripe: ⅝ yard for center block border, zigzag border strips

Gold-and-white stripe: ½ yard for stars

Teal solid: ⅓ yard for stars

Cobalt blue (text print): ⅓ yard for stars

Variety of hot pink, red, and fuchsia prints and solids: 3 yards total for zigzag border strips

Bright green solid: ⅛ yard for center block cornerstones

Small solid scraps: ⅓ yard total for minis

Backing: 8 yards

Batting: 95˝ × 95˝

Binding: included in navy solid yardage (above left)

Center Block

Mini Block

Construction

1. With a variety of bright-colored solid scraps, make 25 minis (1½″ × 1½″) following Parlor Trick Three: Mini Made Fabric (page 77).

2. Sew into 5 rows of 5; then sew the rows together. Press the seam allowances open.

5″ Geese Squared Blocks

CUTTING

Aqua solid

- Cut 4 squares 4⅝″ × 4⅝″; subcut in half diagonally in both directions to make 16 triangles.

- Cut 1 square 8⅜″ × 8⅜″; subcut in half diagonally in both directions to make 4 side setting triangles. *Fig. A*

- Cut 2 squares 4½″ × 4½″; subcut each in half diagonally to make 4 corner setting triangles. *Fig. B*

Bright yellow solid

- Cut 16 squares 2⅝″ × 2⅝″; subcut in half diagonally to make 32 triangles.

White solid

- Cut 4 squares 2¼″ × 2¼″.

Construction

1. Make 4 blocks following the Geese Squared block instructions (page 64) and using the pieces cut for 5″ Geese Squared blocks (above). The unfinished blocks should measure 5½″ × 5½″. *Fig. C*

2. Arrange the Geese Squared blocks, side setting triangles, and corner setting triangles around the

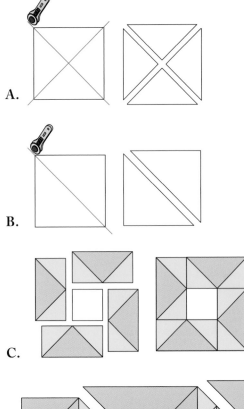

A.

B.

C.

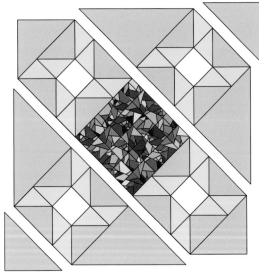

D.

5 × 5 mini block. Sew the blocks and triangles together in diagonal rows; then sew the rows together, pinning at intersections to match points. This center block should measure 14⅝″ × 14⅝″ including seam allowances. *Fig. D*

Center Block Borders and Cornerstones

CUTTING

Navy solid

• Cut 8 strips 1½″ × 14⅝″.

Pink-and-red stripe

• Cut 4 strips 2″ × 14⅝″.

Bright green solid

• Cut 4 squares 4″ × 4″.

Construction

1. Sew a navy strip on both long sides of a pink-and-red strip. Press the seam allowances. Make 4. *Fig. E*

2. Sew one of these units onto one side of the center block. Sew another unit on the opposite side. Press the seam allowances toward the border unit.

3. On the 2 remaining border units, sew a bright green cornerstone to each short end. Press the seam allowances toward the border unit.

4. Pinning at the intersections, sew 1 border/cornerstone unit to a remaining side of the center block. Repeat on the opposite side. Press the seam allowances. *Fig. F*

E.

F.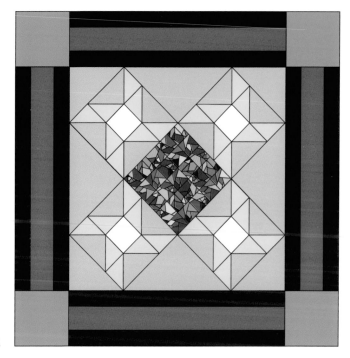

Half-Square Triangle Units

CUTTING

White solid

• Cut 7 squares 6¾″ × 6¾″ for magic 8 half-square triangles.

• Cut 12 squares 3⅜″ × 3⅜″; subcut in half diagonally to make 24 triangles.

Hot pink solid

• Cut 7 squares 6¾″ × 6¾″ for magic 8 half-square triangles.

• Cut 2 squares 3⅜″ × 3⅜″; subcut in half diagonally to make 4 triangles.

Navy solid

• Cut 2 squares 3⅜″ × 3⅜″; subcut in half diagonally to make 4 triangles. *Fig. A*

Magic 8 Half-Square Triangles

Draw a diagonal line in both directions on the back of each white 6¾″ × 6¾″ square. Place each one, right sides together, with a hot pink square. Sew ¼″ away on both sides of each line. Cut apart precisely in the center—vertically, horizontally, and on both diagonal lines—as shown in red on the diagram. Press the seam allowances open. Each set of squares makes 8 half-square triangle units. *Fig. B*

Construction

1. Sew a navy triangle to a hot pink triangle. Press the seam allowances open. Make 4.

2. Trim the dog-ears. Arrange the half-square triangle units and white triangles to form a large triangle unit. *Fig. C*

A.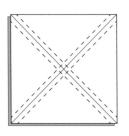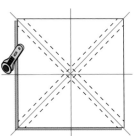

B.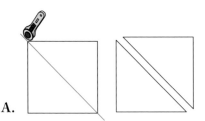

Sew ¼″ away on both sides of diagonal lines.   Cut along red lines, as shown.

C.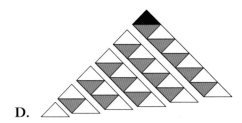

D.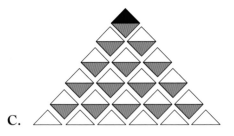

3. Sew together in rows; then sew the rows together, pinning carefully to match the points. *Fig. D*

4. Repeat to make 4 of these large triangle units.

5. Sew the long side of each large triangle unit to the center block borders—to opposite sides first, then to the 2 remaining sides.

Bright Yellow-and-White Braid

CUTTING

Make templates A, B, C, L, and R using the Soigné braid patterns (pages 125–127).

Various yellow solids and tonal prints and white solids

- Cut 24 strips 1¾″ × width of fabric. Subcut into:

4 squares 1¾″ × 1¾″	4 using template C
4 rectangles 1¾″ × 3″	84 using template L
4 rectangles 1¾″ × 4¼″	68 using template R
4 using template B	

- Cut 4 triangles using template A.

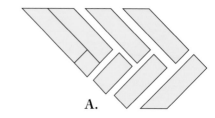

A.

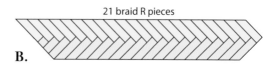

21 braid R pieces

B.

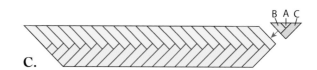

B A C

C.

Construction

Braided Borders

1. Start from the *left* and select 21 braid L pieces, 1 square, 1 each of both sizes of rectangles, and 17 braid R pieces. Be careful not to stretch the bias edges.

2. Beginning with a braid L piece, place a square on the squared end, right sides together. Sew across the end. Open and press the seam allowance toward the square.

3. Place another braid L piece, right sides together, aligning the long side with the top side of the first piece and extending to the end of the square.

4. Sew together with a ¼″ seam, as shown. Open and press the seam allowance up. *Fig. A*

5. Continue with a 1¾″ × 3″ rectangle, then another braid L piece, and then a 1¾″ × 4¼″ rectangle. Press the seam allowances up each time.

6. Continue alternating braid L pieces and braid R pieces. *Fig. B*

7. Repeat Steps 1–6 to make 4 braided borders.

Triangle Braided Corners

1. With right sides together, sew the short side of a braid A piece to the short side of a braid B piece. Press the seam allowance toward A.

2. Sew a braid C piece to the opposite side of the triangle, across the end of B. Press the seam allowance up. Make 4.

3. Sew each braid corner onto the right side of a braided border. *Fig. C*

4. Sew the short side of the braided border onto the quilt. Stop and start sewing ¼″ in from the edge of the pieced center. Press the seam allowances open. Repeat on all 4 sides.

5. Sew the mitered corners of the braid border, pinning at each intersection to match the seams.

Half-Star Triangle Units

CUTTING

Navy solid: Cut 16 using the Soigné diamond D pattern (page 125).

Gold-and-white stripe: Cut 16 using the Soigné diamond D pattern (page 125).

White solid: Cut 16 using the Soigné diamond D pattern (page 125).

Teal solid: Cut 8 using the Soigné diamond D pattern (page 125).

Cobalt blue (text print): Cut 8 using the Soigné diamond D pattern (page 125).

Aqua prints and solids

• Cut 4 squares 9¼″ × 9¼″.

• Cut 2 squares 13⅝″ × 13⅝″; subcut in half diagonally in both directions to make 8 side setting triangles. *Fig. A*

• Cut 4 squares 9⅝″ × 9⅝″; subcut in half diagonally to make 8 end triangles. *Fig. B*

Construction

1. Referring to the quilt photo, place the diamonds D together in sets of 4 to make 16 large diamonds. Sew the diamond sets together, pressing the seam allowances open. *Fig. C*

2. Place 1 diamond right sides together with a side setting triangle (1 and 2 on the diagram). Starting ¼″ from the edge of the inner triangle point, backstitch and sew to the outside edge. Open and press the seam allowance toward the triangle. *Fig. D*

3. Place the diamond/triangle piece on *top* of a second large diamond, right sides together. Start sewing from the bottom point of the diamond. Stop sewing ¼″ from the inner corner (at the intersecting

seam). With the needle in the down position, pivot at the corner, bringing the top of the diamond and the side of the triangle edges together. Continue sewing to the outer edge of the triangle. Press the seam allowance toward the triangle. *Fig. E*

4. Sew 1 setting square to the right-hand side of the second diamond, creating the unit shown in the diagram. Starting ¼″ from the inner point of the diamond, backstitch and sew to the outer edge of the square. Press the seam allowance toward the square.

5. Sew 1 end triangle to the left side of this unit. Press the seam allowance toward the triangle. *Fig. F*

6. Repeat Steps 2 and 3 to make another unit. Sew 1 end triangle to the right side of this unit. *Fig. G*

7. Sew these 2 units together, starting at the star center. Stop with the needle in the down position at the inner corner, and pivot the fabric edges together to continue sewing to the edge of the square, making a half-star triangle unit. *Fig. H*

8. Repeat Steps 2–7 to make 3 more half-star triangle units.

9. With right sides together, align the long side of 1 large triangle star piece with one side of the yellow braid. The ends of both pieces should intersect at the ¼″ seamline. Pin together along the edge, matching the center point of the star to the seam between the twelfth and thirteenth braid strips. Be careful not to stretch the bias edges. Sew. Press the seam allowances toward the star.

10. Continue around the quilt top, pinning and sewing the half-star triangle units to the braid edges. *Fig. I*

A.

B.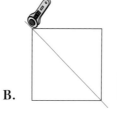

C.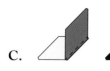

D.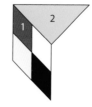

E.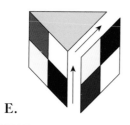

F.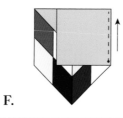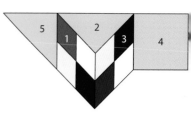

G.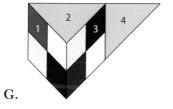

H.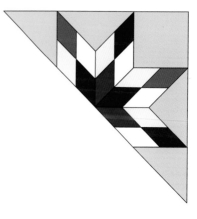

I.

Zigzag Coarse-Woven Border

CUTTING

Various aqua prints and solids

- Cut 17 strips 2⅛″ × width of fabric. Subcut into:

  8 squares 2⅛″ × 2⅛″ (E)

  12 rectangles 2⅛″ × 3¾″ (F)

  28 rectangles 2⅛″ × 5⅜″ (G)

  16 rectangles 2⅛″ × 8⅝″ (H)

  16 rectangles 2⅛″ × 11⅞″ (I)

White solid

- Cut 1 strip 2⅛″ × width of fabric; subcut into 16 squares 2⅛″ × 2⅛″ (J).

Hot pink solids, red solids, and hot pink tonal prints

- Cut 45 strips 2⅛″ × width of fabric. Subcut into:

  172 rectangles 2⅛″ × 8⅝″ (K)

  4 squares 2⅛″ × 2⅛″ (L)

  4 rectangles 2⅛″ × 3¾″ (M)

  4 rectangles 2⅛″ × 5⅜″ (N)

  4 rectangles 2⅛″ × 7″ (O)

Bright yellow

- Cut 2 strips 2⅛″ × width of fabric; subcut 24 squares 2⅛″ × 2⅛″ (P).

Navy solid

- Cut 15 strips 2⅛″ × width of fabric. Subcut into:

  24 rectangles 2⅛″ × 11⅞″ (Q)

  4 rectangles 2⅛″ × 10¼″ (R)

  24 rectangles 2⅛″ × 5⅜″ (S)

  4 rectangles 2⅛″ × 3¾″ (T)

Aqua solid

- Cut 7 strips 2⅛″ × width of fabric. Subcut into:

  24 rectangles 2⅛″ × 8⅝″ (U)

  4 rectangles 2⅛″ × 7″ (V)

Top Left Corner of Border

Work from top to bottom to construct 4 continuous coarse-woven border units.

1. Sew together the strips in order, following the numbers on the diagram. *Fig. A*

2. With right sides together, align a hot pink K strip to the top right of this unit. Sew to about 2″ before the end of the strip and secure with a short backstitch (partial seam). Press lightly away from this new strip (only the part of the strip sewn).

3. Sew a navy Q strip on top of this unit.

4. Sew an aqua E square onto the end of a hot pink K strip. Sew this to the bottom of the row unit, with the aqua square to the right. *Fig. B*

5. *Begin the braid weave.* Sew a hot pink K strip to the bottom, starting with the aqua square end. Sew to about 2″ before the end of the strip and secure with a short backstitch. This is a partial seam. Press the seam toward the top of the row unit. *Fig. C*

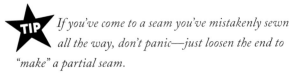 **TIP** *If you've come to a seam you've mistakenly sewn all the way, don't panic—just loosen the end to "make" a partial seam.*

6. Sew the end of an aqua G strip to the end of the vertical hot pink K strip. Then complete the partial seam, sewing the side of G to the rest of the row unit. *Fig. D*

7. Sew another hot pink K strip to the bottom, starting with the aqua end. Sew to about 2″ before the end of the strip and secure with a short backstitch (partial seam). Press the seam toward the top of the row unit.

8. Sew another aqua G strip to the right side of the unit, starting with the newest hot pink K strip end. Sew to about 2″ before the end of the strip (partial seam). Press the seam toward the rest of the row unit. *Fig. E*

9. Repeat Steps 7 and 8 with an additional hot pink K strip and aqua G strip. *Fig. F*

10. Sew a yellow P square onto the end of a hot pink K strip. Then sew this unit to the bottom of the row unit, with the yellow square to the left. *Fig. G*

11. *Change the weave direction.* Sew a hot pink K strip to the bottom, starting with the yellow square end. Sew to about 2″ before the end of the strip and secure with a short backstitch (partial seam). Press the seam toward the top of the row unit. *Fig. H*

12. Sew the side of a navy S strip across the left yellow/pink 3-strip end. Then complete the partial seam above, sewing the end of S to the rest of the row unit. *Fig. I*

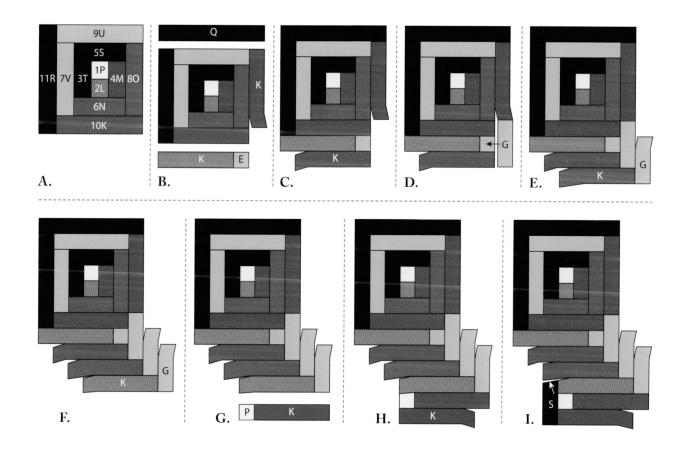

A. B. C. D. E.

F. G. H. I.

13. Sew a hot pink K strip to the bottom, starting with the navy end. Sew to about 2˝ before the end of the strip and secure with a short backstitch (partial seam). *Fig. J*

14. Sew the side of an aqua U strip across the left end of the row unit (keep the overhanging above the K strip out of the way). Then complete the partial seam above, sewing the end of U to the rest of the row unit.

15. Sew another hot pink K strip to the bottom, starting with the aqua end. Sew to about 2˝ before the end of the strip and secure with a short backstitch (partial seam). *Fig. K*

16. Sew the side of a navy Q strip across the left end of the row unit (keep the overhanging above the K strip out of the way). Then complete the partial seam above, sewing the end of Q to the rest of the row unit.

17. Sew a white J square onto the end of a hot pink K strip. Then sew this unit to the bottom of the row unit, with the white square to the right. *Fig. L*

18. *Change the weave direction.* Sew a hot pink K strip to the bottom, starting with the white square end. Sew to about 2˝ before the end of the strip and secure with a short backstitch (partial seam). Press the seam toward top of row unit.

19. Sew an aqua G strip across the right side of the unit, across the white/pink 3-strip end. Then complete the partial seam above, sewing the end of G to the rest of the row unit. *Fig. M*

20. Sew a hot pink K strip to the bottom, starting with the aqua end. Sew to about 2˝ before the end of the strip and secure with a short backstitch (partial seam).

21. Sew the side of an aqua H strip across the right end of the row unit. Then complete the partial seam above, sewing the end of H to the rest of the row unit. *Fig. N*

22. Sew a hot pink K strip to the bottom, starting with the aqua end. Sew to about 2˝ before the end of the strip and secure with a short backstitch (partial seam).

23. Sew the side of an aqua I strip across the right end of the row unit. Then complete the partial seam above, sewing the end of I to the rest of the row unit.

24. Sew a yellow P square onto the end of a hot pink K strip. Then sew this unit to the bottom of the row unit, with the yellow square to the left. *Fig. O*

25. *Change the weave direction.* Continue sewing the strips in this established pattern until the row is completed, ending with an aqua E square and an aqua F strip on the lower right corner of unit.

26. Repeat Steps 1–25, making 3 more of the same coarse-woven border units. *Fig. P*

27. Pin and sew a border onto the top edge of the quilt, starting with the short aqua ends aligned with quilt top edge and leaving the right-hand long end unsewn for about 4˝ (partial seam).

28. Then pin and sew the left side border onto the quilt. The bottom short aqua ends should align with the quilt top, and the top aqua ends should align with the end of the first aqua strip from the top border. *Fig. Q*

29. *Sew the corners together.* Complete the corner's partial seams following the number order on the diagram. *Fig. R*

30. Repeat Steps 28 and 29 to add the remaining borders.

J.

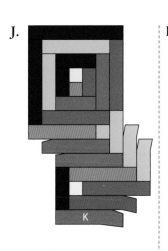

K.

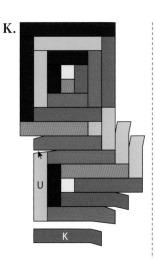

U

K

L.

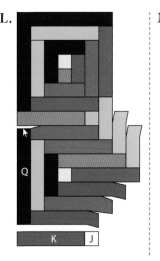

Q

K J

M.

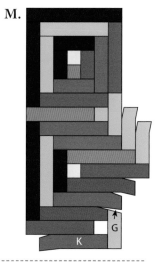

G

K

N.

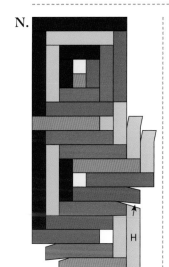

H

K

O.

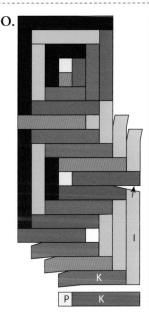

I

K

P K

P.

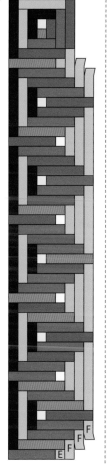

F
F
E F

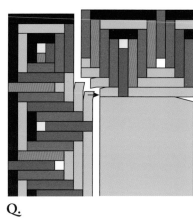

Q.

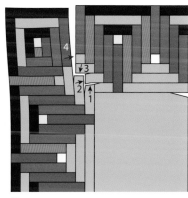

4
3
2
1

R.

Finishing

1. Lightly press the quilt top, being careful not to stretch the fabrics.

2. Layer, quilt, and bind.

PARLOR TRICK FIVE:
FREE-FORM CURVES

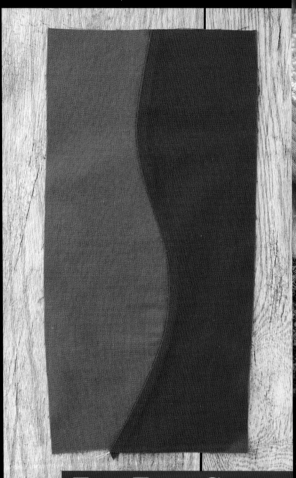

Free-Form Curves

Understanding how a curve works helps take the fear out of learning this next parlor trick. I often hear people say, "Oh, I don't do curves!" I say, "Really? Well, let me show you a fun curve that you can learn in less than fifteen minutes."

CONSTRUCTION

1. Cut rectangles 6½″ × 11¼″ of 2 different fabrics: blue and green in this example.

2. Stack together with both fabrics right sides *up.*

3. With a rotary cutter, cut a shallow free-form curve length-wise through the rectangles.

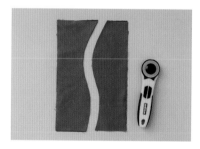

4. Pair the right side of the blue half with the left side of the green half and vice versa, giving you 2 mirror-image sets.

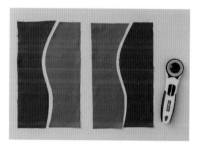

5. Place the first pair right sides together. (They will look completely wrong now.) Align the top edge so the pieces intersect at the ¼″ seamline.

6. With your left hand on the top fabric and right hand on the bottom fabric, sew the curve, keeping the raw edges together as you sew.

TIP *Be careful not to pull either side. Just let the feed dogs take the fabric through the sewing machine as you continue to adjust the raw edges together along the curve.*

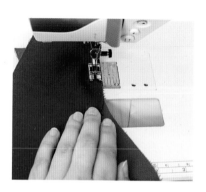

7. Press the seam allowances toward the darker fabric. Trim your block to 5½″ × 10½″.

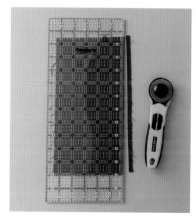

Waverunner, by Victoria Findlay Wolfe, 2009, 49″ × 46″

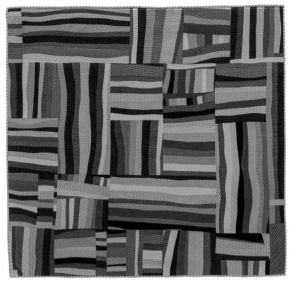

Waverunner II, by Victoria Findlay Wolfe, 2009, 45″ × 45″

Not only is this easy to master but you can also use this one technique to make an entire unique quilt. *Waverunner* was my first foray into playing with curves. I took a giant stack of solids and just started cutting simple wavy curves to make random pieces of wavy curved fabric blocks. Then by cutting them to fit together and squaring them up, I made a very fun quilt without using a pattern.

I was so excited by my first one that I did a quilt-along on my blog and made *Waverunner II* at the same time. You can still see variations of *Waverunner* by doing a quick Internet search. It's always fun to see the many variations of this quilt, whether it's a different choice of colors, length of blocks, or pattern formed from how the waves run together.

The exploration of a technique can bring you to a new relaxed space of creativity by breaking you out of your usual comfort zone of piecing. Cut easy curves, piece, and square up. … Come up with your own beautiful version!

CLASS PROJECT: LOLLING LANDSCAPE

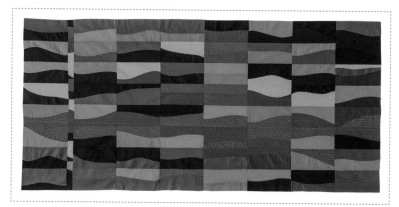

By Victoria Findlay Wolfe, 2016, 81″ × 40″ (before quilting)

MATERIALS

8 or more fabrics: ⅜–⅝ yard of each

Backing: 4 yards

Batting: 87″ × 46″

Binding: ⅝ yard

CUTTING

• Cut a total of 64 rectangles 6½″ × 11¼″.

Using Parlor Trick Five: Free-Form Curves (page 100) to make many quick wavy blocks, I made *Lolling Landscape.* I let the blocks guide me and tell me what my design would be, and, selecting a pile of solids and one print, I set out to make some blocks. I would decide afterwards how I wanted to put them together.

As soon as I laid them out on my design wall, I saw the relaxed shapes of a gently rolling landscape. The blocks could have lived in any formation to be an interesting abstract, but I decided to use my intuition on what I saw in the blocks. I made three extras to finish the design.

At the very end of the process, I decided to use everything I had trimmed off. As a treat in my quilt (and to fix that one thing that was not quite right), I added my small cut-off trimmings to the design, which draw my eye to them and give the quilt vertical and horizontal movement.

This class project should be an exploration of improvisation and free-form curves.

Make the Blocks

1. Follow Free-Form Curves, Construction (page 101) to make 64 free-form curve blocks.

2. Set aside the pieces left over from trimming the blocks.

Construct the Quilt

1. Arrange the blocks in an 8 × 8 grid or however you wish. Remember this is an improvisational quilt!

2. Sew the blocks together into vertical rows.

3. Sew together the trimmed pieces to make a strip 1½″ × 40½″.

4. Sew the strip between 2 rows of blocks.

5. Finish sewing the rows together.

Finishing

1. Lightly press the quilt top, being careful not to stretch the fabrics.

2. Layer, quilt, and bind.

THE DIFFERENCE
BETWEEN THINGS

Finished quilt: 88˝ × 95˝ (before quilting)

I had another idea … how would curves within the blocks look if I tried the partially seamed herringbone pattern? I quickly took a few extra scraps, made a few blocks, stuck them to my wall, and instantly saw its potential! *The Difference between Things* became a quilt top in two days—I was on a mission.

 The title is often an interesting story. When I made this quilt, I felt like I was looking at Matisse cutouts. I have a favorite quote by Matisse; he said, "I don't paint things. I only paint the difference between things." I think that quote sums up the way I look at quilt patterns. Just because a pattern was designed to look a certain way doesn't mean that's the way it has to be. Look at each individual shape and view it as an opportunity to *play* with the information, color, or pattern within that particular shape. You might be pleasantly surprised!

In this case, I sure was. And even better, my husband came into the studio and said, "Matisse—it looks like Matisse!"

I said, "Yes! I think so, too." (Nailed it!)

MATERIALS

Yardage amounts are given for each fabric to be used in two adjacent rows. To create the interwoven effect, each fabric is paired in the left-leaning blocks with one color and in the right-leaning blocks with another.

If you want to repeat a fabric for a second braid, double the yardage amount for that fabric. For added movement in the quilt, I used two different prints in similar colors for some of the braids.

Configuration: 29 blocks × 5 rows (+ 2 half-rows)

Braids: 1⅛ yards each of 12 fabrics

Side setting triangles: ¾ yard

Backing: 8 yards

Batting: 94″ × 101″

Binding: ⅞ yard

CUTTING

Braids: Cut 15 rectangles 6½″ × 11¼″ from each fabric. (Each rectangle will make 2 curved pieces.)

Side setting triangles: Cut 7 squares 8⅜″ × 8⅜″; subcut diagonally in both directions to make 28 side setting triangles. *Fig. A*

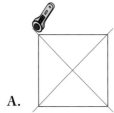

A.

Make Free-Form Curve Blocks

1. Select 1 turquoise and 1 red rectangle (or whichever color combination you choose), and stack both fabrics together right sides *up*. With a rotary cutter, cut a shallow free-form curve lengthwise through the rectangles. *Fig. B*

B.

2. Pair the right-side turquoise half with the left-side red half and vice versa, giving you 2 mirror-image sets. *Fig. C*

3. Sew the curve sets together, following Parlor Trick Five: Free-Form Curves (page 100).

4. Press the seam allowances to the darker fabric. Trim the block to 5½″ × 10½″.

C.

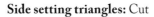

By Victoria Findlay Wolfe, quilted by Kelly Cline, 2016

5. Repeat with 7 additional pairs of the same fabrics, playing with different curves. Make 15 blocks. (Since each pair of rectangles makes 2 blocks, you will have 1 extra curve set to play with in another project!)

6. Continue to the next curve-block fabric pairs—red and light orange. Make free-form curve blocks with 7 pairs of rectangles for a total of 14 blocks.

7. Using the full quilt photo as reference, continue making the free-form curve blocks in the fabric pairs needed. The left-leaning sides require 15 blocks; the right-leaning sides require 14 blocks.

Make the Half-Row Units

1. Units for the left edge of quilt: Sew a side setting triangle to the left short side of a turquoise/red curve block. Make sure the turquoise half is positioned on the bottom of each block. *Fig. D*

2. Units for the right edge of quilt: Sew a side setting triangle to the right short side of a turquoise/orange curve block. Make sure the turquoise half is positioned on the bottom of each block. *Fig. E*

Construct the Rows

Work from the bottom to sew the curve blocks needed for each row. Follow the row layout diagram for the color layout and the direction of each block. Fig. F

1. With right sides together and the ends aligned, sew the short end of a left-leaning block to the side of a right-leaning block, forming an L. Continue with the row. Follow the directions for Parlor Trick One: Partial-Seam Construction (page 13).

2. Add alternating blocks, using 15 left-leaning and 14 right-leaning blocks. These are all partial seams. Each seam should be open on the outside edges, about 2˝ from the end, and the seam allowances should be pressed up.

3. Sew the 4 remaining rows. Start at the bottom of each row with a left-leaning block each time.

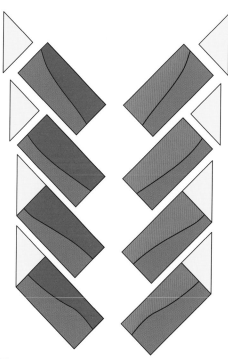

D. Make 14 units.　　**E.** Make 13 units.

F. Row layout for queen-size quilt

Add the Half-Row Units

You will be adding blocks with setting triangles, working from the *top* of the row down.

1. Sew the end of the turquoise/red curve block (*without* the side setting triangle) to the side of the top right-leaning block in row 1. *Fig. G*

2. Lay another turquoise/red curve block (*with* the side setting triangle) right sides together with the bottom of the first block and aligned with the end of the top row 1 block. Sew across, keeping the remaining row 1 blocks out of the way. *Fig. H*

3. Open and finger-press the seam allowances up (toward the top of the rows).

4. Fold *down* these blocks and the top strip on row 1. Finish this partial seam, keeping the remaining strips out of the way.

TIP *It can help to place a pin in the intersecting seam allowance to hold it in the correct direction as you sew the new seam.*

5. Open and finger-press the seam allowance up.

6. Repeat Steps 2–5 until 15 turquoise/red curve blocks are added.

7. Similarly, sew the turquoise/orange curve blocks to the right side of row 5. Start by sewing the side of a turquoise/orange curve block (*without* the side

setting triangle) to the end of the top left-leaning curve block in row 5. *Fig. I*

8. Open and finger-press the seam allowance up.

9. Fold down these top blocks and finish the partial seam, keeping the remaining strips out of the way. Open and finger-press the seam allowance up.

10. Continue down the row, first sewing the side of a turquoise/orange curve block (*with* the side setting triangle) to the bottom of the first block, aligning the end of the turquoise/orange curve block with the end of second block in row 5. Then complete the partial seam across the end of this new block, and so on, until 14 turquoise/orange curve blocks are added.

Join the Rows

You will be working from the *top* of the rows down, joining and completing the partial seams.

1. Follow Herringbone, Join the Rows (page 16).

2. Trim the top and bottom edges even with the innermost points. *Fig. J*

Finishing

1. Lightly press the quilt top, being careful not to stretch the fabrics.

2. Layer, quilt, and bind.

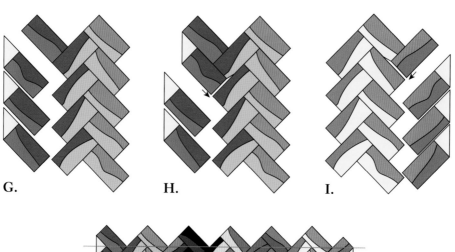

G.   H.   I.

J.

ADDITIONAL SIZES

Fabrics	Crib (45″ × 60″)	Twin (74″ × 88″)	Queen (88″ × 95″)	King (102″ × 95″)
Configuration	19 blocks × 2 rows (+ 2 half-rows)	27 blocks × 4 rows (+ 2 half-rows)	29 blocks × 5 rows (+ 2 half-rows)	29 blocks × 6 rows (+ 2 half-rows)
Braids	⅞ yard each of 6 fabrics	1⅛ yards each of 10 fabrics	1⅛ yards each of 12 fabrics	1⅛ yards each of 14 fabrics
Side setting triangles	¾ yard	¾ yard	¾ yard	¾ yard
Backing	3 yards	5½ yards	8 yards	8½ yards
Batting	52″ × 66″	80″ × 94″	94″ × 101″	108″ × 101″
Binding	½ yard	¾ yard	⅞ yard	⅞ yard

CASCADE

Finished quilt: 76″ × 92″ (before quilting)

Once you understand the trick of piecing free-form curves, piecing template curves becomes a breeze. Keeping the centers aligned so the mirror image is not disturbed, pin the center and then the outside edges. Three pins is all you need. This works whether you are piecing Double Wedding Rings or Drunkard Path blocks. Always pin your centers!

When making this quilt, I used the curve to give the simple braid technique a powerful twist. Bias is always an issue with curves, and this quilt is no different. Even when taking care to pin the center and edges, you will still have a stretchy top. The

rows help keep it in check, but for visual effect, sometimes a quilter has to do what a quilter has to do for a beautiful-looking quilt.

I chose two fat-quarter bundles of a similar palette and decided to make them work as one for this gradational quilt. I infused solids as a way to help direct the gradation, by making the solid relate to what sat next to it in a light or dark nature. I also wanted to change up the pattern by having the color placement form arcs or V's across the design of the quilt, so I could create more movement in a repeating pattern.

By Victoria Findlay Wolfe, quilted by Shelly Pagliai, 2016

MATERIALS

This is a scrappy quilt, so fabric amounts vary and the yardage is approximate. A selection of light to dark fat quarters plus some additional blacks and whites are all you need to create this gradational color beauty. (About 87 different prints/solids were used.)

Fabrics	Crib (38″ × 60½″)	Twin (76 × 92″)	Full (85½″ × 92″)	Queen (95″ × 102½″)	King (114″ × 102½″)
Row layout	39 curve strips × 4 rows	57 curve strips × 8 rows	57 curve strips × 9 rows	63 curve strips × 10 rows	63 curve strips × 12 rows
Light to dark prints and solids	3 yards total	8½ yards total	9½ yards total	11½ yards total	13 yards total
White/off-white solids	1½ yards total	3¾ yards total	4½ yards total	5½ yards total	6 yards total
Black solid	½ yard	1 yard	1¼ yards	1½ yards	1½ yards
Backing	2½ yards	7 yards	7¾ yards	8½ yards	10 yards
Batting	44″ × 67″	82″ × 98″	92″ × 98″	101″ × 109″	120″ × 109″
Binding	½ yard	⅞ yard	⅞ yard	⅞ yard	1 yard

CUTTING

Make templates using the Cascade left- and right-side curve strip patterns (pages 126 and 127).

Fabric*	Crib	Twin	Full	Queen	King
Left-side curve strip template	78	228	256	315	378
Right-side curve strip template	78	228	257	315	378

This is the exact number of strips needed for each size layout, but it is useful to cut extras so you can play with color. I started by cutting out 2 left-side and 2 right-side curve strips from each fat quarter I had chosen; then I started playing with the pieces on my design wall, moving and filling in where needed.

NOTE > Use the pattern pieces provided to cut the left-side and right-side curve strip pieces. Use a pencil or chalk pencil to transfer the two pattern marks on the long edges of each piece. These marks will make it easy to align curves when sewing.

Arrange the Pieces

On a design wall (or the floor), arrange the pieces to create a gradational effect. I started with pairs of left and right curves from the same fabrics in an arc. Then I played with some, making matching pairs into V's and filling in with other single curves. Use the photo as a reference and have fun seeing how your fabrics work together from dark to light and back again!

Construct the Rows

The approximate finished row width is 9½˝. You will be working from the bottom, *alternating the right- and left-side curves to build each row.*

NOTE > The ends of the strips are dog-eared to help with aligning the edges. As you add each strip, you will sew across the end and side of the previous strips. Pin at the beginning, the end, and at the marks on the long edges. This is a gentle curve, so you will want to be careful not to straighten it out. As you sew, make sure you keep the raw edges together along the edges of the curved strip. Don't pull the fabric—allow the feed dogs of your sewing machine to take the fabric through.

1. With right sides together and the ends aligned, sew the short end of a *right*-side curved strip to the side of a *left*-side curved strip. *Fig. A*

2. Flip open and press (or finger-press) the seam allowance up.

3. With right sides together, sew another right-side curved strip to the right/top side of the unit.

4. Flip open and press the seam allowance up. *Fig. B*

5. In the same way as Steps 3 and 4, continue adding left- and right-side curved strips until the row reaches the number of strips needed for the desired layout. The sides of your rows should be aligned and the edges straight. *Fig. C*

6. The next row is constructed similarly but is a mirror-image layout. For this row, begin by sewing the short end of a *left*-side curved strip to the side of a *right*-side curved strip. *Fig. D*

A.

B.

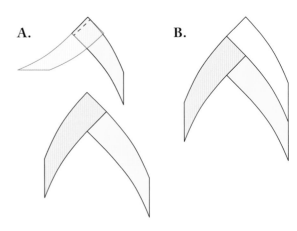

C.

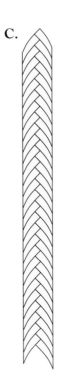

D.

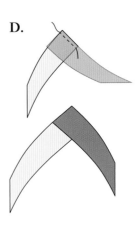

7. Continue adding left-and right-side curved pieces until the row reaches the number of strips needed for the desired layout. *Fig. E*

8. Make the remaining rows, remembering to alternate the starting curved strip (right-side, then left-side) every other row. See the layout diagram for reference.

Join the Rows

1. Starting from the left side of the quilt, pick up the first 2 rows. With right sides together, pin at each intersection. It's a lot of pinning for each row, but this will ensure your points match well in the end! Sew this long straight seam carefully so you don't stretch the fabrics.

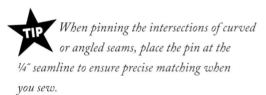 *When pinning the intersections of curved or angled seams, place the pin at the ¼″ seamline to ensure precise matching when you sew.*

2. Sew the remaining rows together in pairs; then sew the pairs together until you've completed the quilt top.

3. Press the long seam allowances open. Some steam helps everything lie flat. Lightly press the quilt top, being careful not to stretch the fabrics.

4. Lining up with a long ruler, trim the top and bottom edges even with the innermost points. *Fig. F*

Finishing

1. Lightly press the quilt top, being careful not to stretch the fabrics.

2. Layer, quilt, and bind.

E.

F. Row layout for twin-size quilt

COLORING DESIGN PAGES

Herringbone

Coarse Woven

LeMoyne Star

Soigné

Free-Form Curves

Cascade

PATTERNS

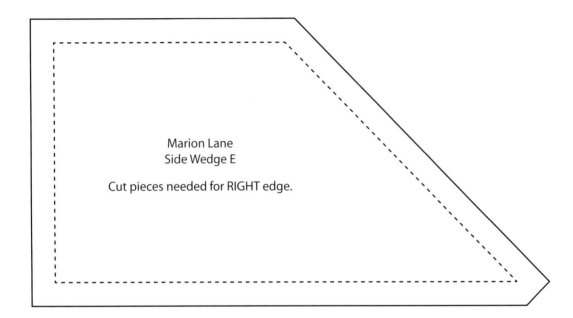

Marion Lane
Side Wedge E

Cut pieces needed for RIGHT edge.

Use a ruler to measure
these inch marks to verify that
printout is correctly sized.

1″

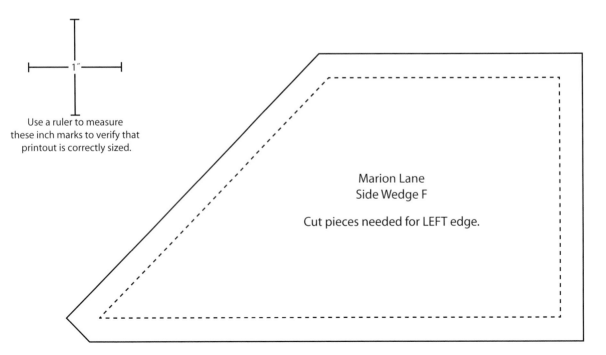

Marion Lane
Side Wedge F

Cut pieces needed for LEFT edge.

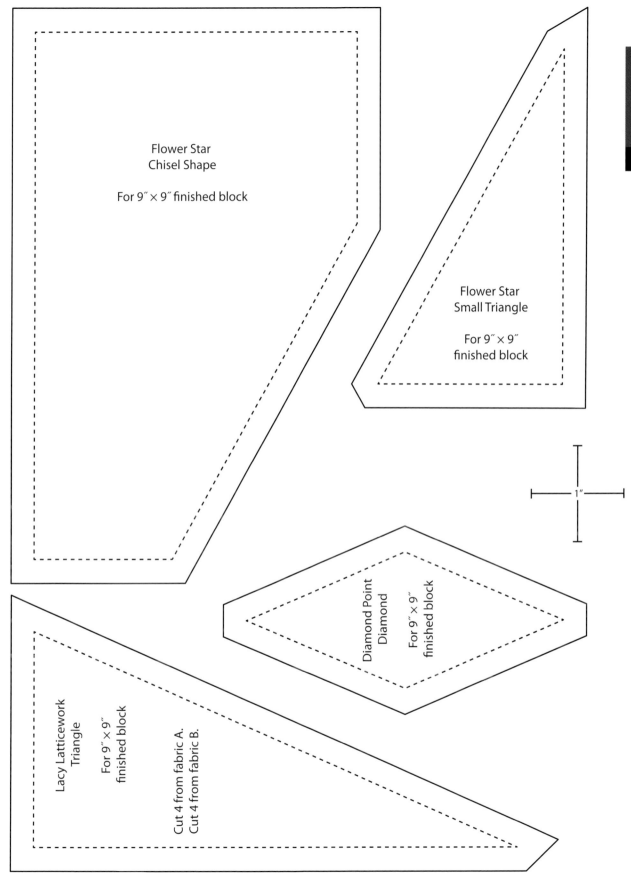

Flower Star
Chisel Shape

For 9″ × 9″ finished block

Flower Star
Small Triangle

For 9″ × 9″
finished block

1″

Diamond Point
Diamond

For 9″ × 9″
finished block

Lacy Latticework
Triangle

For 9″ × 9″
finished block

Cut 4 from fabric A.
Cut 4 from fabric B.

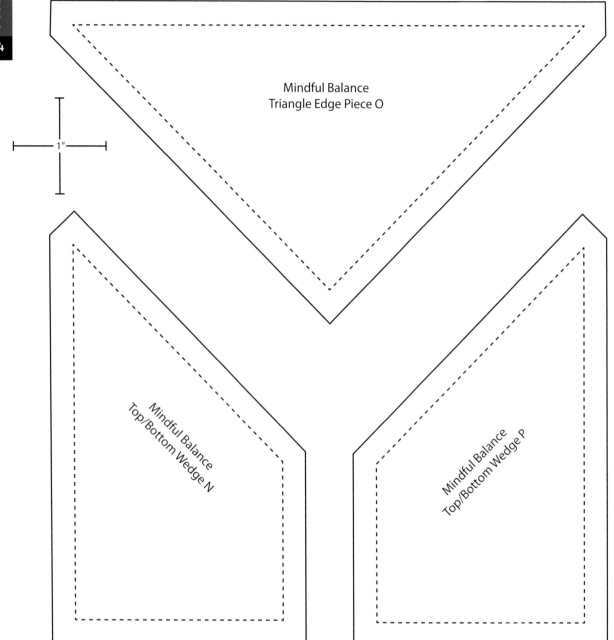

Mindful Balance
Triangle Edge Piece O

1"

Mindful Balance
Top/Bottom Wedge N

Mindful Balance
Top/Bottom Wedge P

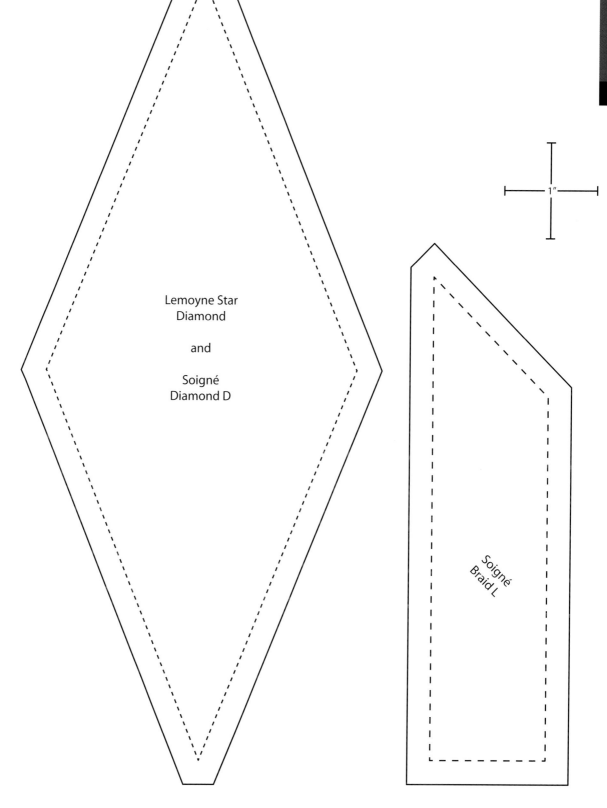

Lemoyne Star
Diamond

and

Soigné
Diamond D

Soigné
Braid L

1"

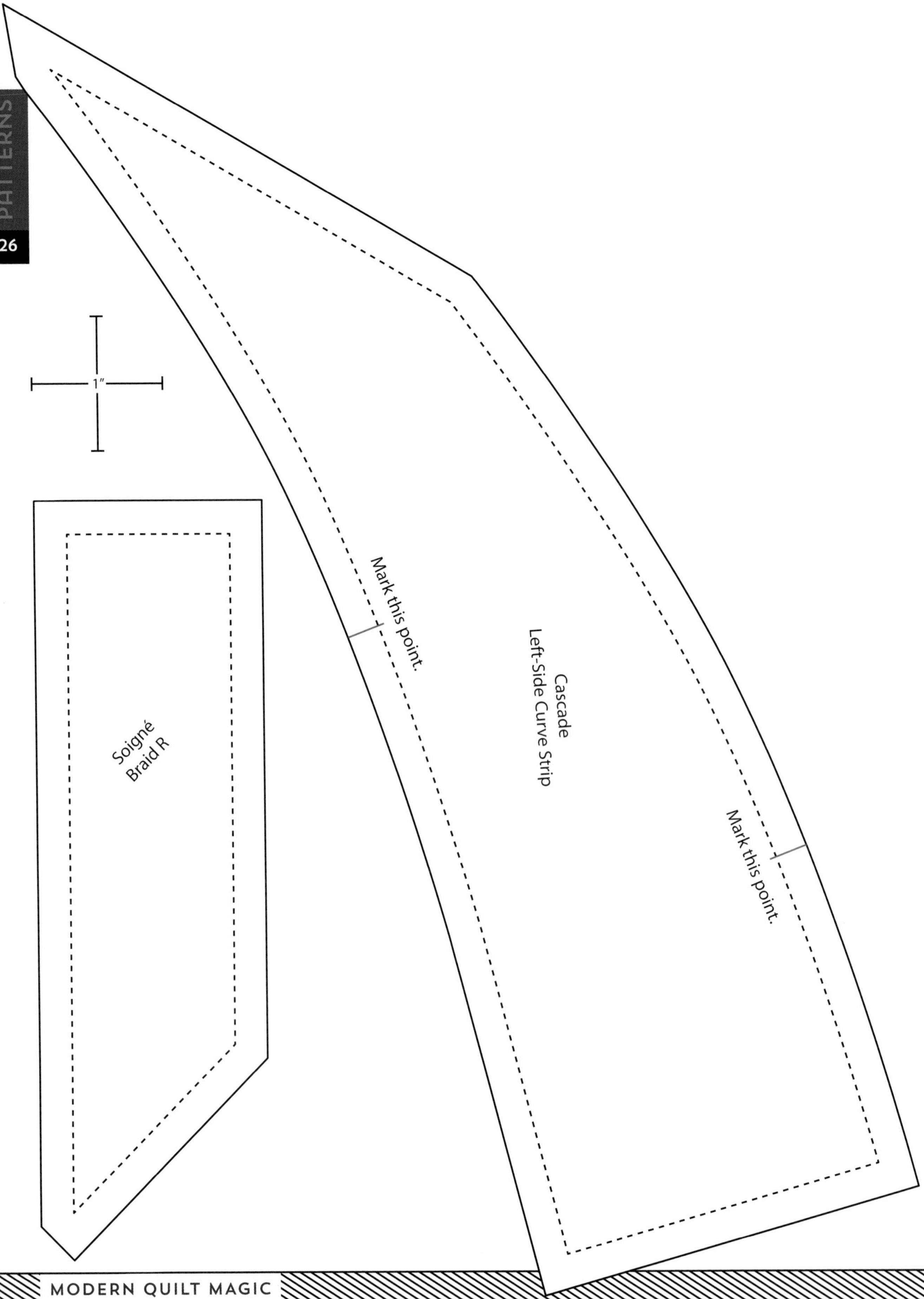

1"

Soigné
Braid R

Cascade
Left-Side Curve Strip

Mark this point.

Mark this point.

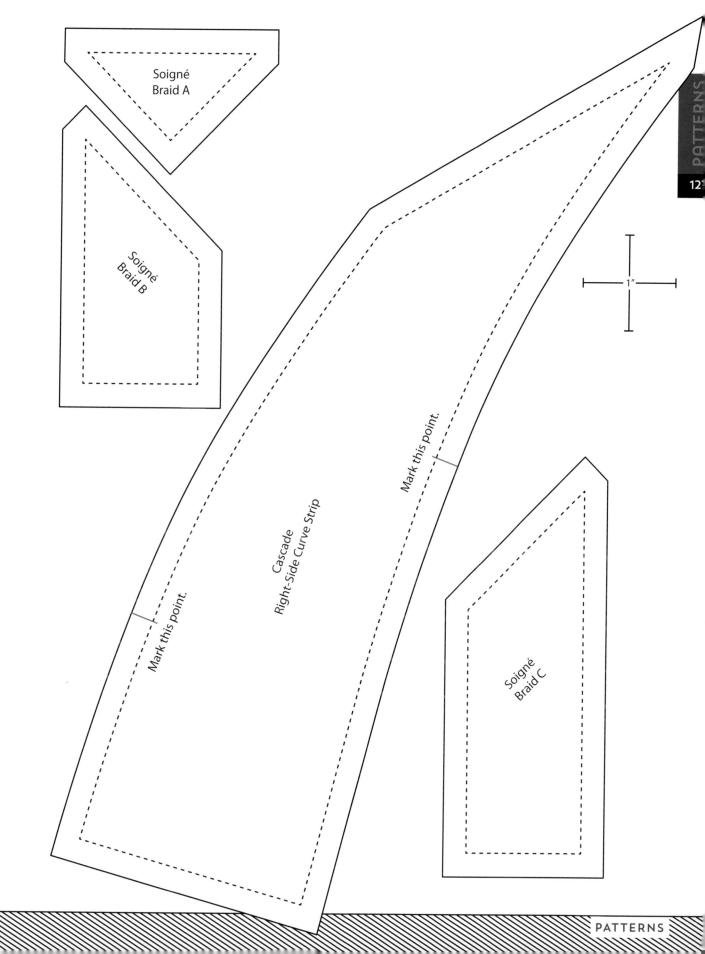

Soigné
Braid A

Soigné
Braid B

Soigné
Braid C

Cascade
Right-Side Curve Strip

Mark this point.

Mark this point.

1"

ABOUT THE AUTHOR

Victoria Findlay Wolfe is a New York City–based award-winning quilter, international teacher, lecturer, and author of *15 Minutes of Play—Improvisational Quilts* and *Double Wedding Ring Quilts—Traditions Made Modern* (by C&T Publishing). Victoria also designs fabrics for Marcus Fabrics and is a licensed designer for Sizzix die cuts and Aurifil thread sets. She is the Juki U.S.A Ambassador and has created her own acrylic template line, available at her website.

She is active behind the scenes of the quilt world, as well, with the Quilt Alliance, the Wisconsin Museum of Quilts & Fiber Arts, and as an advisory board member of the International Quilt Study Center & Museum. She runs her own community-based quilt drive through BumbleBeansBasics.com, as she feels that giving one quilt for each one you make is the best gift of all. Victoria's quilts have been exhibited internationally; she loves to teach and share the fun of quilting without fear to quilters all over the globe.

Born and raised on a farm in Minnesota, Victoria credits her quilting influences to her grandmother's double-knit polyester crazy quilts that kept her warm growing up. Her biggest supporters are her husband and daughter.

Visit Victoria's website for information on products, guild visits, and exhibits at vfwquilts.com. Or visit her VFW Quilts NYC store: 325 West 38th Street, Suite 811, New York, NY 10018. (Check her website for the most current address.)

For more inspiration and ideas, visit www.15minutesplay.com.

Instagram: @VictoriaFindlayWolfe

Facebook: Victoria Findlay Wolfe Quilts